THE WAY WE GET BY

BY NEIL LaBUTE

★

★

DRAMATISTS
PLAY SERVICE
INC.

THE WAY WE GET BY
Copyright © 2016, Neil LaBute

All Rights Reserved

SPECIAL NOTE

SPECIAL NOTE ON SONGS AND RECORDINGS

THE WAY WE GET BY was originally produced by Second Stage Theatre (Carole Rothman, Artistic Director; Casey Reitz, Executive Director), New York City, on April 28, 2015. It was directed by Leigh Silverman, the scenic design was by Neil Patel, the costume design was by Emily Rebholz, the lighting design was by Matt Frey, the sound design was by Bart Fasbender, the production stage manager was David H. Lurie, and the stage manager was Amanda Kosack. The cast was as follows:

BETH .... Amanda Seyfried
DOUG .... Thomas Sadoski

CHARACTERS

BETH

DOUG

A slash ("/") indicates where the present speaker stops and the next speaker begins.

"It is never too late to be what you might have been."
—George Eliot

"We were together. I forget the rest."
—Walt Whitman

"I give her all my love, that's all I do."
—The Beatles

THE WAY WE GET BY

The beginning.

An apartment in New York. A nice one. Someone has been living here for a while now and things are piled up in that way that they get when you're starting to run out of places to put stuff.

It all looks good and is very ordered, but it's feeling a bit crowded in the corners.

The windows are dark. Nighttime out. The sound of light traffic.

After a moment, a guy wanders on in his underwear and a sweatshirt. He's nice-looking in his own way. Pretty fit but doesn't seem to care about it much. This is Doug.

He wanders over to the fridge and opens the door. Looks inside. Grabs a bottle of water and opens it. Chugs two or three good gulps out of it and then carries it back into the living area.

He plops down onto a couch and spreads out. Feet up on the coffee table. Picks up a book and opens it. Reads a line or two, makes a face, tosses it back onto a stack.

He grabs a remote and turns on the TV. The sound of it blasts on loudly. It's on the QVC channel and someone is selling purses or clothes or some damn thing.

Doug quickly turns it off and puts down the controller. He glances over his shoulder at the hallway. Waits.

After another beat, he seems to relax and picks up one more book.

Cracks it open and starts to read. He finds something funny and laughs out loud.

Doug reaches over, snaps on a lamp and sits back to do a bit more reading. Takes another sip of water.

A young woman appears in the hallway. Looking out. She wears a Star Wars *t-shirt but otherwise seems pretty naked. This is Beth.*

Doug smiles again at something in the book. Laughs out loud. Beth keeps watching him.

BETH. ... Not great to wake up alone. *(Doug snaps his head around and jumps up. Drops the book on the couch and looks over at Beth.)*
DOUG. Hey. Sorry about that.
BETH. Yeah, no, it's okay. Just weird.
DOUG. I know. Right. That's ... not ...
BETH. I thought maybe you left or something.
DOUG. No! *(Beat.)* Of course not ... no.
BETH. I mean, I see that now but at the time I was just, like — a few seconds ago I'm saying — I got all freaked out ... / Not *super*-freaked, but ... you know ... "ish." *Freakish.*
DOUG. I understand. / I get it.
BETH. Okay. Good.
DOUG. But that's ... *(He gestures.)* ...
BETH. Sorry?
DOUG. No, nothing ... I just ... I mean, you have my shirt on there ... so ... *(Beth looks down. Stretches out the logo to read it.)*
BETH. Oh.
DOUG. Yeah. I wouldn't leave without that! It's *vintage* ... It's not, like, from *Target* or something. I got it at Comic Con. *(Beat.)* Kenny Baker? The little guy who played the robot? R2-D2? He signed it. *(Points.)* Right there. Above your ... yep.
BETH. I'm ... I didn't realize that. *(He waves her off. Adjusts his underwear a little bit.)*
DOUG. No problem. You're welcome to wear it. *(Beat.)* But that should've been a clue ... no way I'm leaving without that!
BETH. I just ... sorry, no ... I just grabbed the first thing I felt on

the floor and put it on. / Sorry.

DOUG. That's fine ... / No, it's all good ...

BETH. I wasn't suggesting ... you know. I don't even like *Star Wars* that much ... so I wouldn't *steal* it or anything!

DOUG. Great. *(Smiles.) I'll* keep it then.

BETH. Cool!

DOUG. Uh-huh. *(The two of them stand there in silence for a moment. Beth looking around, still waking up.)*

BETH. Did you turn on the TV or something? / Oh. I thought I heard the ...

DOUG. Ummmmmm, no. Not the ... / Uh-uh. *(Pointing toward a book.)* I was just ... reading ...

BETH. Huh. Okay.

DOUG. Yep. *(Beat.)* Not "reading" but *browsing* ... *(Beat.)* TV's just sitting right over there on the shelf thingie. Unused. *(Beat.)* Yep. "Console"? Is that what they call it? Not a *shelf thingie.* "Console," I think ... *(Another moment of quiet. He holds out the water for Beth.)* You want some? I woke up and I was, like, *so* thirsty so I just ... Hope it's alright.

BETH. Sure. *(Looking.)* It doesn't say "Kim" on there, does it?

DOUG. *(Turning it over.)* Nope. It's just ... "Smart Water" is all it says. *(Shows her.)* See?

BETH. Okay, good. *(Beat.)* My roommate writes her name on everything she buys — her food, I mean — she basically buys the same stuff as me and then she ... whatever ... she gets pissed if I use any of it, even if it's mine. So I was just ... you know ... *(Points.)* Curious.

DOUG. No, yeah, that makes sense. *(Looks again.)* This one appears to be yours.

BETH. Good.

DOUG. Sorry again ... I should've asked.

BETH. No, it's totally ... you know ... *community property* or whatever. / I'm fine with it.

DOUG. Thanks. / I would've checked with you first but you were pretty zonked out.

BETH. I understand.

DOUG. That'd be funny, though ... if she did.

BETH. What?

DOUG. Sorry ... I just mean, what you said a second ago ... about your roommate.

BETH. Kim?

9

DOUG. Yeah. If she did put her name on *all* her stuff … not just her food, I'm saying … but, like, the *couch*, or, or, or if she bought that rug there or something …

BETH. That actually *is* her rug …

DOUG. Oh. 'Course. *(Doug looks at the rug for a moment, then around the rest of the apartment. Looks back at Beth, who says:)*

BETH. Yep. *(Pointing.)* That lamp there, too. And the coffee table. Shelves, as well. *(Beat.)* Pretty much everything you can see …

DOUG. Huh.

BETH. *(Looking around.)* That *vase* is mine.

DOUG. Nice! You have *really* good taste …

BETH. Actually, she bought it for me. / Kim.

DOUG. Oh. / Wow.

BETH. Yeah. I mean, it had flowers and stuff in it at the time — for my birthday — but yes, Kim picked it out.

DOUG. I see.

BETH. I think she got it so it'd match the rest of her things, but … that's just me …

DOUG. No, yeah, I bet you're right … *(He looks around.)* Pretty good match, too!

BETH. *See?*

DOUG. No, I get it. *(Beat.)* Anyhow, that's what I mean. What if she went around and put her name on things, like in these *huge* letters … everything that was hers…? *(Beat.)* Like, with a *stencil? (Doug mimes what he means, pretending to write out the name "Kim" in massive letters on the couch first and then the rug and a few other furnishings.)*

BETH. I wouldn't put it past her! *(Doug stops and smiles at her. They look at each other.)*

DOUG. Sounds like it. *(Beat.)* Wouldn't that be crazy, though? If she did that?

BETH. That'd be funny.

DOUG. Right? "KIM." *(Beat.)* I wonder if anybody has ever done that in, like, the history of roommates? *(Beat.)* You think?

BETH. Probably.

DOUG. Yeah. No doubt.

BETH. I know people have come up with a lot of wild stuff in those situations … masking tape down the middle of rooms and, like, cutting things in half. / Seriously.

DOUG. True. / Yeah. *(Beat.)* Probably not masking tape, though.

BETH. Excuse me.

DOUG. Oh, nothing, no … just … I'm saying it's probably not *masking* tape they use, in a case like that. *(Beat.)* Wouldn't stick so good …

BETH. No?

DOUG. I don't think so.

BETH. Oh.

DOUG. Probably more like duct tape.

BETH. "Duck" tape?

DOUG. Yeah. "Duct." With a "t." / "Duct."

BETH. Oh. Okay. / Got it. "Duc*t*."

DOUG. You know what that is … the silver kind?

BETH. I guess.

DOUG. No, you've seen it before. Now they have all kinds — different colors, I'm saying, or zebra stripes — but it used to be just silver and it was for big jobs. Plumbing and that type of thing. Construction. Or packing boxes. *(Beat.)* You know? *Silver* …

BETH. I think so. Yeah. I've seen it before … I feel like we have some around here. The silvery kind. Or gray. Ish. *Grayish. (Beat.)* Right? *(Doug shrugs and nods. Thinking about it for a moment.)*

DOUG. Yeah. Anyway, it was probably from all of the … like … wine or maybe the … We did some whiskey, too, didn't we? I remember doing something … Was it *whiskey*?

BETH. What're you … I'm not sure what you mean now?

DOUG. Oh, sorry! Yeah, I jump around a lot of the time … my mind does … that's a little bit of a problem with me these days.

BETH. Oh.

DOUG. It wasn't always when I was younger but it is now. Not a *problem* … but … a thing I do. / My brain does. Whatever.

BETH. Huh. / I see.

DOUG. Yep. *(Beat.)* I went back to the thing from before … reason that you fell asleep last night so quick. *(Beat.)* After we … *(Beat.)* You know … *(Beat.)* Yeah. *(Beat.)* Yep.

BETH. Got it.

DOUG. Good.

BETH. I see.

DOUG. Yeah. That's what I meant. That you had a lot to drink — no judgement, we both did — and that's why you were sleeping that way before. So soundly.

BETH. … Maybe so …

DOUG. Anyway, you were asleep, you were really out of it and I just felt like I should let you rest … so …

BETH. That makes sense.

DOUG. Right?

BETH. Sure. Thanks for that. I get it now.

DOUG. Yeah, and I … but I would never just go like that. Take off. / Without letting you know first or, like, saying goodbye. I really wouldn't … I'm not that guy … the "sneak out after *you-know-what* guy." That isn't me. *(Beat.)* Nope.

BETH. That's nice. / Thank you.

DOUG. Especially without my shirt there!

BETH. Right! *(Laughs.)* But like I said, I didn't know it was yours at the time … so …

DOUG. Yeah, no, I get it. That's true. *(Another moment of silence. A siren in the distance. Doug is still standing and he takes a step toward Beth as he holds out the bottle of water.)* Sure you don't want a sip? Apparently it makes you "smart" or something …

BETH. Ha! I don't think that's the case …

DOUG. I dunno. It says so, right here … *(He points to the label.)* "Smart Water." I don't think they can *lie* about that …

BETH. No. Probably not. *(Smiles.)* You wanna … What're you thinking? Did you want to go, or … you wanna come back in? / To bed now, or … just … you tell me.

DOUG. Oh. / Ummmmmmmmm … *(She waits for him to say something more but he doesn't.)*

BETH. Awkward. *(Beat.)* No *pressure.* I was just asking …

DOUG. Right, no, no, no, that's … I'm just …

BETH. I'm not making a big deal out of it or anything …

DOUG. … I understand … I get that …

BETH. If you need to go, you can … Go for it. Now's your chance …

DOUG. No, it's not *that* … / ummmmmm …

BETH. So then…? / What?

DOUG. I just … I'm kinda awake now. I know it's early but I feel like I'm up … so like I probably can't sleep again. / For a while.

BETH. Oh. / Okay. *(Beat.)* That's okay. If you're not tired … then … *(Beat.)* I didn't just mean for "sleep." Necessarily.

DOUG. Ahhhhh. I see. *(Beat.)* But *you* should … you do need your sleep so don't let me stop you from … you know …

BETH. No, I'm fine …

DOUG. Yeah, but you probably … you're working tomorrow, right? Didn't you say that to me … last night … up at the…?

BETH. I do. I mean, I did, yes, I said that … at the thing. Right.
I did. Meaning yes, I do. I'm working tomorrow. *(Beat.)* Yep.
DOUG. Uh-huh. *(Beat.) Today*, technically.
BETH. Right! *(Doug checks his watch. Yes, he still wears a watch.)*
DOUG. In just a little bit …
BETH. True. *(Yawns.)* I actually should get a couple more hours …
but …
DOUG. Go ahead. No problem. I'm off today, but …
BETH. Okay. So … does that mean…? *(Beat.)* What exactly does
that mean, though? For us … here. You and me …
DOUG. Nothing.
BETH. "Nothing." *(Beat.)* So … what does *nothing* mean? You
wanna leave?
DOUG. No! Not at all … I can hang out here.
BETH. Yeah? / While I'm sleeping?
DOUG. Yep. / Totally. *(Beat.)* We could even go get breakfast or
something. Before you work. Or whatever. *(Beat.)* I'd do that …
BETH. You *wanna* do that?
DOUG. I *can*, absolutely … or … or … *(Doug is trying to negotiate
this moment very carefully.)* Okay, look … I'll be honest with you …
I never expected this to happen! Between us? Not *ever*!
BETH. Me either.
DOUG. Yeah, so, it's just … I mean, shit! I'm just a little caught
off-guard here, so, you know … just …
BETH. I agree. I'm not even *processing* it right now … I'm just
going with it …
DOUG. … okay …
BETH. So, it's better that way. *(Beat.)* You can get back into bed if
you want to … if that's not too … OR … you can go, I guess …
DOUG. Yeah, but if I can't sleep and I start to get all … you know …
(He demonstrates just how restless he might get in bed.)
BETH. *(Smiling.)* Okay, okay … if you're gonna be like that —
epileptic — then no. / That would suck.
DOUG. Ha! / Yeah. I'm a *really* light sleeper …
BETH. Me, too. *(Beat.) Super* light.
DOUG. I remember that.
BETH. Oh. *(Beat.)* You do?
DOUG. Yep. I mean, I think so … kind of.
BETH. That's … huh. Okay. *(Beat.)* Really?
DOUG. Maybe not. *(Shrugs.)* I dunno! *(Doug smiles and nods.*

Waits. Beth smiles and nods too.)
BETH. I mean … that was a while ago.
DOUG. Pretty long ago now. That's true.
BETH. Right.
DOUG. But I sorta do remember that. For some reason … your whole "sleep" deal.
BETH. Huh. *(Beat.)* It's a pretty recent thing.
DOUG. Okay, maybe not. *(Beat.)* I'm not sure now.
BETH. Okay. Cool. *(Beat.)* So … you wanna just hang out here? Watch TV or something? We have HBO but not Showtime … in case there's some series you like or whatnot. *(Points to his t-shirt.)* *Game of Thrones* or one of those … I'm guessing.
DOUG. Ha! No, I'm totally good! *(Smiling.)* I'm not really into shows about *dragons* … / Wookies are cool, but no dragons! *(Beat.)* It's complicated.
BETH. No? / Okay, then maybe you wanna just finish that *TV Guide* there? / Or keep "browsing"? *(She points at the volume that Doug had been perusing when she entered the room. He laughs at this. Picks it up.)*
DOUG. Yeah, maybe! / Why not? *(Reading.) Are You There Vodka, It's Me, Chelsea. (Beat.)* That's the one chick from on TV, right?
BETH. Uh-huh. The blonde one.
DOUG. Right. *(Beat.)* She's funny.
BETH. You think?
DOUG. Kinda. Dirty-funny, but yeah. She's okay. *(Beth nods quietly but doesn't seem to agree. Doug puts the book back down and steps away from the coffee table.)*
BETH. I don't like her that much. *(Beat.)* Lots of people do — Kim does — but I don't.
DOUG. No?
BETH. Uh-uh. She thinks she's really clever and cute and all that, like, you know … cuter than she actually is … I mean, she's cute but not *that* cute. / Not, like, *adorable.*
DOUG. Yeah. / No, I know what you mean …
BETH. And I hate that in people. Especially in girls. *(Beat.)* My roommate's like that and I don't care for it … that "I'm *such* a cutie" attitude.
DOUG. "Kim," you mean? Or…?
BETH. Yeah. *Kim.* She's totally like that.
DOUG. Huh. *(Beat.)* Cool.

BETH. What?

DOUG. Sorry?

BETH. What's so "cool" about that? I mean … what's great about being that way? *(Doug shrugs and says nothing. Beth watches him. Waiting.)*

DOUG. No, nothing! Just that … you said "roommate" so I'm guessing you only have one, is that right? / You share this apartment with just one other person?

BETH. … yes … / Yeah. Kim.

DOUG. So that's what I meant by "cool." I think it's nice when you have a place almost to yourself and not a bunch of other people. Sometimes it's great to just have the run of a place and not feel like you're … you know … *some* …

BETH. No, I get what you mean. / I do.

DOUG. Yeah? / Okay, then.

BETH. Sure. *(Beth laughs to herself at this. Looks around and steps a bit further into the living room. She crosses into the kitchen area. Opens the fridge door.)*

DOUG. Sorry. Sometimes I can just get talking and I look up and, like … *two hours* have somehow passed! Stupid, really …

BETH. No, it's fine.

DOUG. Yeah?

BETH. Absolutely. *(Beat.)* Nice to have someone around who … you know …

DOUG. What?

BETH. No, nothing.

DOUG. … wears awesome t-shirts?

BETH. Ha! *(Pointing.)* Yes!! You can't have too many of these Darth Vadar logos around for my taste! They just *reek* of class … *(Doug laughs at this. Takes another drink from the bottle of water and then caps it. Beth closes the fridge door.)*

DOUG. Hey, hey! That shirt is amazing — and lots of people like *Star Wars*! Women, too … *(Beat.)* Probably less than guys … but I think a lot do. Enjoy Sci-Fi, anyway.

BETH. … I *know* …

DOUG. Alright then. *(Beat.)* It's not childish. *Star Wars* is awesome … there's a whole mythology there. *Hero with a Thousand Faces*? Joseph Campbell? Kurosawa's *Hidden Fortress*? No? *(Beat.)* Anyway, yeah, I've had a few bumps on the road to growing up … I'm the *first* to admit that … but …

BETH. Ha! And I'd be the second hand up on that one …

DOUG. Hey! / Come on now! / Ouch! *(Doug pretends to get an "arrow to the heart." He stumbles backward, holding his chest. Beth smiles at his antics.)*

BETH. I'm kidding! *Sort of.* / "Ish." / Let's just put it this way: You haven't exactly been in a *hurry* to become an adult …

DOUG. No, that's true … but, you know … why should I be? What's the point of that?

BETH. I dunno. I guess it's what we're supposed to do, right? / Isn't that what people are always saying?

DOUG. I guess. / Anyhow … whatever …

BETH. Whatever is right. Do what you want. If wearing this thing makes you happy, then go for it. / *(Points to shirt.)* It's fine.

DOUG. *Thank you.* / 'ppreciate it.

BETH. Not really my place to judge …

DOUG. That's kinda true as well.

BETH. Won't *stop* me … but it's not really my place!

DOUG. Ha! Right! *(They share a smile and a little laugh at this. Doug looks around, noticing that he's not wearing much more than his underwear and a sweatshirt.)* I should … probably … you know. At least put my pants on, though.

BETH. I mean … if you're uncomfortable … / Don't worry about it for *me*, but … sure.

DOUG. No, but … / What if your roomie comes back? What's her name again? "Kim"? I don't wanna throw her into a *tizzy* …

BETH. True. *(Thinks.)* She's not supposed to … at least I think so. She's staying over at her boyfriend's place tonight. *(Beat.)* This is Sunday, right? / So … yeah …

DOUG. Uh-huh … / Well, technically Monday now, but, it was Sunday just a little bit ago.

BETH. That's what I meant. Last night. *(Doug nods at this and glances at his watch. It is in fact after midnight so yes: It's now Monday.)*

DOUG. Sure. 'Course. *(Checks his wrist.)* Last night it was Sunday night … *(Pointing to his watch.)* Calendar.

BETH. Thank you. *(Beat.)* So what are we doing here … *(Beat.)* You know what? Here … *(Before Doug can offer any resistance, Beth pulls off the* Star Wars *shirt and reveals her body. Lovely, ordinary, and kind of perfect. A young woman naked.)*

DOUG. No … wait … that's … *okay* … *(She tosses the shirt to him and disappears down the hall for a minute. Doug pulls off his sweatshirt and puts on the* Star Wars *shirt and looks around. He sits back and waits. About to pull on his sweatshirt when Beth returns wearing a v-neck t-shirt and a tiny pair of panties. Some socks pulled up to her thighs as well. She poses for him.)* Nice!

BETH. Yeah ... sexy, right? *(Doug laughs but doesn't say anything. Beth sits down next to him on the couch. It's quiet for a few beats.)*

DOUG. Actually, yeah. I like that look. *(Mimes.)* With the ... what ... the stripes? Like you have there. / Very '70s. Or something ...

BETH. Thanks. / Got 'em at American Apparel. / They're kinda "in" right now.

DOUG. Huh. / Cool.

BETH. You ever been in there?

DOUG. Ummmmm ... yeah. *(Beat.)* Once or twice.

BETH. *Yeah?*

DOUG. Not on my own! / But ... yeah. I have.

BETH. Okay! / I wasn't *judging* you ...

DOUG. I know, but ... they don't have too much stuff for guys ... but some things ... hats ...

BETH. Sure. *(Smiling.)* Were you in there with a girl?

DOUG. That's not ... come on now!

BETH. I'm just asking!

DOUG. I know, but ... *God* ... we just ... you know?

BETH. I'm not asking *who* — her name or anything like that — just if I'm right or not.

DOUG. Okay. Yes. *(Beat.)* A girl.

BETH. Your ex?

DOUG. ... yes.

BETH. I see.

DOUG. It's not ... no. Nothing.

BETH. No, what?

DOUG. Not my last one — *Whitney,* not her — but the one before that.

BETH. Oh. *(Beat.)* Who?

DOUG. I don't think you ever met her ...

BETH. Yeah, but what's her name? *(Doug shrugs and hesitates but finally looks up and over at Beth. Smiles and says:)*

DOUG. Pamela. *(Beat.)* She went by "Pam" mostly but yeah ... her name was Pamela.

BETH. Hmmm. *(Beat.)* The blonde girl?

DOUG. Nope ...

BETH. Not "blonde" but, like, dirty blonde … with the bangs…? Kinda like my hair?

DOUG. Not her, either. A different one.

BETH. Oh.

DOUG. Anyway, it was her. *Pam.* I went with her.

BETH. Got it. *(Beat.)* I don't remember her.

DOUG. That's what I said …

BETH. No, right, and I'm just agreeing with you about it. I never met any "Pam" or, like, "Pamela" or anybody like that …

DOUG. Well, we didn't go out that long.

BETH. No?

DOUG. Not at all. Couple months. If that.

BETH. Hmmm.

DOUG. Might even be less than that. *Two.*

BETH. I see.

DOUG. Yeah. *(Beat.)* She was diabetic. *(Beat.)* Not important …

BETH. But she's the one who you went to the store with at some point … right?

DOUG. Yep. Somewhere in there … during our *few* dates or whatever … between radical dips in her blood sugar levels … we went in. *(Beth seems ready to pursue this a bit further but it's clear that Doug is more than finished with the subject so she decides to drop it.)*

BETH. He's kind of a perv … right?

DOUG. Sorry?

BETH. The guy who ran that place. Owned it. / Have you heard about him? He even got arrested.

DOUG. Oh. I dunno. / No. Did he?

BETH. I'm pretty sure. I think he actually got fired. From his own company. *(Beat.)* You've seen the ads for it before, right? On the back of … you know … *The Village Voice* and places like that?

DOUG. … ummmmmmmm …

BETH. I'm sure you have! They're all over the streets …

DOUG. I think so. *(Beat.)* With the … girls…?

BETH. Yeah, well, supposedly he shoots all of them himself. With people he picks up at the beach or wherever. At the mall. / Out *roller-skating* or that kinda thing …

DOUG. No … / *Really*?

BETH. Uh-huh.

DOUG. Wow.

BETH. Yeah … and then brings them back to his place or to the …

whatever … the *basement* of one of his stores … like, the nearest one … with a *mattress* on the floor …

DOUG. Ha! Did you *read* about this or something?

BETH. No, but everybody says it happens! People have written articles about it …

DOUG. Yeah, no, I'm not doubting you. *(Smiling.)* But it didn't happen to *you*, though … did it? / Just asking! / I thought maybe that's how you got those socks there …

BETH. What?! / *No!* / Idiot! *(She laughs and then looks around the apartment, jumping up to rummage through a stack of papers in a nearby bin.)* I'm sure we've got it … if Kim hasn't thrown it out yet. *(Looking.)* God! I feel like I *just* saw one this morning! *(Beat.)* Where is it…?

DOUG. That's okay …

BETH. I know, but I want you to see what I'm saying … / The photos …

DOUG. … okay … / If you wanna …

BETH. It's alright, I'm sure we have one here somewhere …

DOUG. Seriously, Beth, I can look it up on my phone or … like … my laptop …

BETH. I know, but now it's frustrating me! It was, like, literally ten *hours* ago … and now it's gone … *(Digging.)* I'll find it!

DOUG. Great … I mean, if it's right there …

BETH. It was, but now it's … Kim could probably subliminally tell I might want it tonight so she threw it out! / Seriously wouldn't be surprised …

DOUG. Ha! Can't wait to meet her! / Sounds like a real charmer, this "Kim" …

BETH. Oh yeah! She's … amazing … *(Beth turns and smiles at Doug as she continues to rummage through the papers. After a moment, she turns back around and looks at Doug.)*

DOUG. *What?*

BETH. Are you staring at my ass?

DOUG. … ummmmmmmm …

BETH. Are you?

DOUG. No … that's not … I mean … I wouldn't call it "staring" exactly. / More like "appreciating" it, that's all …

BETH. No? / You *can*, I mean, no law against it or anything, but … I just …

DOUG. What?

BETH. … just kinda wanna know what you're up to back there. Fantasy-wise …

DOUG. Okay, so yes! That was pretty much it. Me *staring*. I was doing the, you know … *(He points.)* Superman thing. / X-ray vision.

BETH. Cool. / Alright. *(Beat.)* That's all … *(She smiles over at him mischievously and then goes back to digging through the papers. Ass turned back toward him again and thrust up in the air a bit. Doug tries not to watch her but it's a losing battle he is waging.)* A-ha! *(She stands up, triumphantly holding up a magazine. Young girl posing in undies and high socks on the back page.)* See? (Beth returns to the couch with* The Village Voice *in her hands. She tosses it onto Doug's lap and then points to the ad in question.)*

DOUG. Yeah. Huh. Look at that … *(Scanning it.)* That's seriously not *you*? / *(Holds it up.)* Turn around again for a second …

BETH. Shut up! / STOP!

DOUG. I'm kidding! *(Looks again.)* Yeah … it's just like you described it. Basically.

BETH. Degrading, right?

DOUG. Ummmmm … yeah. Pretty much.

BETH. "Pretty much"?

DOUG. I mean, she's cute, but … and weirdly … dressed just like *you* …

BETH. Yeah, but … that's *not* the point! *(Beat.)* Right?

DOUG. No, I'm just … saying …

BETH. Either way, it's kinda gross, I think … and I'm not a prude or anything.

DOUG. No, you're *not*.

BETH. I mean … obviously.

DOUG. Right.

BETH. But I just think advertising has gone too far lately. / It's ridiculous! I mean, it really has … *look* at her!! Up on her … *hands* …

DOUG. True. / No, you're right … yeah …

BETH. You know?

DOUG. Yes. Absolutely. *(Beat.)* Although it does seem to be working … this "advertising" thing. *(Smiles.)* But no, you're right. It is gross.

BETH. Ha! *(Slugs him on the arm.)* / You don't feel like that at all!

DOUG. Oww! / No, I do … come on … I do, but … she *is* pretty, though …

BETH. So *what*?! She's *seven*!

DOUG. No!

BETH. She's honestly like seven years old …

DOUG. That's … you're joking, right? / Because she's got great tits for *seven* …

BETH. Yes, of course I am! / Stop! / She's *very* young, though. / A teenager.

DOUG. I'm KIDDING! / Yeah, she is. / That's true.

BETH. Okay then.

DOUG. And that's not the right way for them to sell socks to people. With child labor.

BETH. No, not just — It's exploitative. It's degrading.

DOUG. No, you're right.

BETH. And kinda gross, right?

DOUG. Yeah. Definitely that. "Gross." Girls doing naked handstands are gross … *(Reaches for the magazine.)* Let me just see it one more time to be sure … *(He picks up the ad and pretends to study it very closely. Beth turns and studies Doug for a moment — he has a little grin on his face which is very hard to read. Suddenly she grabs the magazine and rolls it up. Smacking him with it. Doug laughs and fights back. First by holding his hands up to protect himself and then finally being proactive — grabbing at Beth and stopping her any way he can. Together they laugh and keep playing. The "fighting" is slowly giving way to kissing. Real and passionate and hot. A long stream of warm kisses on the mouth and neck.)*

BETH. You're a good kisser …

DOUG. You too.

BETH. I like it … I mean, it's nice … I *really* like kissing you.

DOUG. Agreed. And God … you're *so* beautiful. / Is that okay to say? I mean …

BETH. *Thanks.* / Sure. *(Beat.)* I always knew you would be. Good at kissing. / Yep. I was sure of it … I even *heard* that you were.

DOUG. Yeah? / *Really?*

BETH. Yes. From a few people …

DOUG. So … you thought about it before? I mean, before now? Doing this?

BETH. Of course! Hundreds of times.

DOUG. Yeah? Me, too.

BETH. Seriously?

DOUG. Sure. Maybe not "hundreds," but — *(Grins.)* I'm kidding, but yes, I always imagined that it'd be very nice to kiss *me* … *(Beth now realizes that he's still playing around and she laughs, smacking*

21

him again with the magazine.)
BETH. You're *so* dumb …
DOUG. I *know*! *(Kissing her.)* You too, though.
BETH. Yeah. Kinda. With the right person I can be. A little bit silly …
DOUG. "Silly" is nice. I love "silly."
BETH. Playful.
DOUG. Yes.
BETH. It's good. Right? *(Beat.)* To be that way?
DOUG. Yep. *(They begin to kiss again. Plopping down on the couch and going at it. Suddenly Beth begins to kiss down Doug's neck and across his bare chest. Moving lower. Doug is playing with Beth's hair, letting her go further while he watches her. After a moment, she starts to pull down his underpants — not off but down and out of the way. She looks up at him and smiles, then starts to put his cock in her mouth. Just at the last second, Doug stops her. Pulls her up to look at her and then kisses her again. Several times. Beth is happy to kiss him but curious. Very curious.)*
BETH. … are you … Did you just *stop* me?
DOUG. Hmmmmm?
BETH. … I'm just asking …
DOUG. *What?*
BETH. Did you not want me to … you know…?
DOUG. No! That's not … I just felt like kissing you again. I like that, so … I was …
BETH. … okay …
DOUG. That's all.
BETH. Yeah, but … I mean … I had you, like, *in* my mouth just now …
DOUG. Ummmmmm …
BETH. You were "in" there. / *In*side.
DOUG. No … / But not, like, completely …
BETH. So … do you not like that? That's all I'm asking. / I wanna be *really* clear on that.
DOUG. Ahhhhh … / Okay. *(Beth straightens up now and climbs off Doug. Slumps onto the couch next to him. Doug pulls up his underwear and sits back next to her. They are quiet for a few moments. Glancing at each other.)*
BETH. Is it the shirt?
DOUG. Sorry?

BETH. The t-shirt there ... do you not wanna get ... *stuff* ... on it or something? / You know! Your "stuff" stuff ...

DOUG. *What?* / Are you seriously asking me that?

BETH. ... *well* ...

DOUG. No! *(Beat.)* It's not that.

BETH. I mean, you were all "it's vintage" and like that earlier, so I thought maybe ...

DOUG. Beth, come *on!*

BETH. I'm just asking!

DOUG. Okay, so "no" then, it's not that ...

BETH. 'Cause you can take it off if you want. / I mean, if it's a *sanity* issue ...

DOUG. Please. / ... you mean "sanitary"?

BETH. God! *Don't* correct me right now! / I mean, shit ... don't fucking DO THAT!!

DOUG. Okay, *fine.* / Beth, come *on* ... don't be all — *(He makes an angry face and shakes his hands.)* You know? Jesus ...

BETH. I'm not mad, I'm really not...! It pisses me off but I'm not "mad"! Okay?! There's a difference!!

DOUG. Yeah? You kinda sound like you are. *Mad.*

BETH. Well, I'm not!! / Fine. / Good.

DOUG. Alright. / Cool. / You sure? *(They steal glances at each other for a minute. Silence.)*

BETH. I am *honestly* not mad, so please don't keep saying that ... that I am.

DOUG. I'm not.

BETH. Yeah, but you were ... just now. Like, *one* second ago ...

DOUG. I didn't say that, though. That you were *mad.* / Not that word.

BETH. Fine. / Okay, but ...

DOUG. I just think you're sorta put off by the fact that I ... whatever ...

BETH. You stopped me. *(Beat.)* In motion.

DOUG. I just ...

BETH. No, you *stopped* me with your ... thing ... basically *within* my mouth.

DOUG. It wasn't *in.*

BETH. Ummmmm, *excuse* me, but ... yeah ...

DOUG. ... it was just ... on the *edge* ... / Or, like, the *rim* ...

BETH. Hey, I was there! / Right there!

DOUG. Okay, *fine* ... then yes, it was in ... but, like ... just

23

barely …

BETH. "Barely" is in! That's "in" the mouth. / Your tip was fully inside of my mouth cavity … so …

DOUG. Fine. / Okay.

BETH. Yeah. "Okay."

DOUG. I'm not gonna argue about this … because it's not worth it …

BETH. Good.

DOUG. I'm not. It's stupid.

BETH. Don't.

DOUG. I won't.

BETH. *Good.*

DOUG. I'm just saying …

BETH. *What?* What is it, Doug? Tell me … lemme know why you let me pull your undies down and stick your *penis* in my mouth — after we already got pretty crazy earlier in my bedroom, by the way — and now you suddenly stopped me cold … *(Beat.)* So … yeah. Please. Do tell.

DOUG. Okay. *(Beat.)* Because.

BETH. … *because…? (Beat.)* Can we *elaborate* here … please?

DOUG. *Because* I just wanted us to … you know … think it through. / *This.* Doing this here.

BETH. What? / Which part?

DOUG. Come *on*! *(Beat.)* Having sex. Together.

BETH. Ahhhhh … sorry, but we did that already. We had a *lot* of sex earlier tonight, so that's … not the …

DOUG. I know … I know!

BETH. Okay, great! Thought maybe you missed that!

DOUG. Of course not! *Please!*

BETH. … *well* …

DOUG. Look … Beth … I don't wanna fight here … seriously, you know I don't. *(He suddenly stands up and moves away from Beth. Starts to move around the room.)* I just suddenly … you know … I felt the need for us to hold up for a second and just examine this. What we're doing — to think it through. That's all. Assess the damage and just … / Not "damage," but — okay?

BETH. Damage? / Great.

DOUG. So it's not some big "thing" against *you*. My stopping us.

BETH. Well … sure felt like it.

DOUG. It's not! *(Beat.)* I like you … you know that … I *think* you do, anyway … if you don't then now you do. *(Beat.)* I do. I like you, Beth.

BETH. Thank you.

DOUG. Welcome. *(Doug waits for a response. Beth remains quiet so he says:)* I'm … just … I'm knocked out by what happened tonight, I am, but I just feel like we gotta take one step back now and be sensible here. *(Beat.)* We *have* to.

BETH. There's nothing wrong with it.

DOUG. No, I know, I know that … but …

BETH. It just happened.

DOUG. Yes.

BETH. And I wanted it to happen. I *did.*

DOUG. Me, too …

BETH. You sure?

DOUG. Yes.

BETH. I mean for "sure" sure?

DOUG. Of course! / Beth, I've thought about —

BETH. Not of course … / If it was "of course" we wouldn't be on this subject right now, I'd be doing the thing I was doing or we'd be back in the bedroom and all that … if it was so "of course" so no, it's *not* just "of course." *(Beat.)* Okay?

DOUG. Maybe that's true.

BETH. Yeah … so …

DOUG. But if you're asking if I regret what we did here tonight … then my answer is *no. (Beat.)* Is that what you're asking?

BETH. No.

DOUG. But … yeah, it kinda is.

BETH. Kinda.

DOUG. Alright, thank you … and "no" is my answer. I have no regrets about that. None. *(Grins.)* It was fantastic … and you know it was … but I guess I just wanna be sure that … if we *did* do it again … / I dunno. That we …

BETH. What? / …

DOUG. That we really *think* about it! That's all! *(Beat.)* I don't want us to make a mistake here or, or … just … a … not a "mistake" but, you know … once is just an accident, once is a "gimme" and we can walk away, but twice is, like, that's a pattern, that's where the idea of a mistake can come in …

BETH. *Thanks.*

DOUG. I'm not saying it was a mistake! God no!

BETH. Ummmmmm, kinda, yeah! Sounds like it!

DOUG. I said I *liked* it the first time …

BETH. "Liked."

DOUG. Okay, fine, loved it! I *loved* it! *Better?*

BETH. Ummmmmm, yeah. *Lots* better.

DOUG. So then I *loved* it. *(Beat.)* Like I said before … no regrets …

BETH. Okay, good. You have no regrets … you still made me feel bad.

DOUG. That's not … I didn't mean for that to happen! Obviously not!

BETH. Nothing is *obvious* at a time like this, okay? So just …

DOUG. Alright, true. Fair enough. *(Beat.)* I do not wanna rush this is all … blow it or, like … my chance with you. *This* is the part that people usually rush through just to "get off" but I don't wanna do that this time. *(Beat.)* I was actually being cautious for *you* … like a gentleman would do. *(Beat.)* So there. *(Doug stops fidgeting. Sits on the arm of the couch. Beth looks up at him. Shrugs. Silence for a beat or two.)*

BETH. Fine. *(Beat.)* … would you like me better if I did one of those *handstands*?

DOUG. Ha!

BETH. I'm serious! Maybe that's what you guys like …

DOUG. Whoa, whoa, whoa … wait a minute … wait. What's that? Who're "you guys"?

BETH. Just … guys. Guys like you.

DOUG. Hey, that's … there aren't any guys like me out there. Anywhere. *(Beat.)* You know that.

BETH. … I guess …

DOUG. No, you *know* it. That's why you're *here*.

BETH. I live here.

DOUG. You know what I mean!

BETH. Fine. Yes. *(Beat.)* You're unique …

DOUG. I am, yeah. I am. And so are you …

BETH. Fine. We both are. *(Beat.)* So what?

DOUG. "So what" is that this happened to us … it's crazy and amazing and, like, such good sex … right? / Like, *insane* good.

BETH. Yep. / *Pretty* good.

DOUG. Hey! Come on! Play fair …

BETH. Okay, yes. It was. Nice. / Alright! It was "great."

DOUG. "Nice"? / Right, it was great, AND maybe this was always gonna happen and it finally just did …

BETH. Kinda seems like it. *(Beat.)* Doesn't it?

DOUG. Yeah. I mean, that's what I just said … it happened and I really loved it and all that ... *but* ...

BETH. *What?*

DOUG. I'm just ... I dunno! I don't know how to describe it, what I'm trying to say ... I'm a guy ...

BETH. Just say what you're feeling.

DOUG. Oh yeah! Right! *(Smiles.)* I forgot about *that* option ... the *truth.* Good one ...

BETH. Just tell me what's up with you. *(Beat.)* Doug.

DOUG. Okay, okay, okay ... *truth* is ... full disclosure ... *(Doug stops himself. Thinks for a moment, then turns back to Beth.)* Yes. I did turn on the TV earlier.

BETH. *What?*

DOUG. You know ... when you asked earlier ... if I put the TV on and I said "no." That wasn't true. I did do that.

BETH. You did?

DOUG. Yeah. *(Beat.)* See? Told you my mind backtracks ...

BETH. Oh.

DOUG. I just ... Didn't wanna be the one to wake you up or whatever, so I just ...

BETH. You fibbed.

DOUG. Yep. Basically.

BETH. Okay. *(Beat.)* I *thought* so ...

DOUG. It was just for a second, though ... some shopping show was on and I turned it off again. In, like, two seconds.

BETH. I see. / Kim watches that crap.

DOUG. Yeah. / Oh. *(Beat.)* Anyway ...

BETH. It's alright.

DOUG. Yeah, but I didn't need to lie about it.

BETH. That's true.

DOUG. It was just ... you know ... instinct.

BETH. "Instinct"?

DOUG. Or habit or ... I don't mean it's a *habit.* I don't make it a habit to lie, I just ...

BETH. I mean, I never thought you were a liar before ... back in the day or whenever ...

DOUG. I wasn't.

BETH. I'd remember it if you were, because I hate liars.

DOUG. I'm not! *(Beat.)* This is frustrating, okay, because I'm not like this amazing social speaker ... at *all* ... / Not that you can tell ...

BETH. I get it. / Ha!

DOUG. … but I'm *really* trying here, to be an honest person with you …

BETH. No, I appreciate that.

DOUG. Okay, cool, … so … I just blurted it out because … you know … I didn't wanna get in trouble or anything … and it was none of my business, to be messing with your stuff like that, anyway … so I just …

BETH. You lied. / For a second.

DOUG. Yes. / For a second … and I'm sorry.

BETH. No problem.

DOUG. Great.

BETH. It's really not an issue …

DOUG. Thank you!

BETH. And it's not mine, anyway …

DOUG. What's that?

BETH. The TV.

DOUG. Oh. *(Realizing.)* "Kim" again?

BETH. You got it!

DOUG. Ha! Of course! / "Shocker!"

BETH. Yep! / And she never lets me forget it, trust me …

DOUG. How?

BETH. Just … Like with all her crap in here! She just points it out all the time. In her little ways. Little bossy ways.

DOUG. Really?

BETH. Yeah. Just … makes a viewing schedule and won't let me DVR anything without asking first … / "Permission."

DOUG. Wow. / Damn.

BETH. So, yeah … just stuff. Stupid stuff but it bugs me. *(Beat.)* Can't open the fucking windows without asking first. Can't touch her new Urban Outfitters stereo. *Stuff. (Beat.)* See, it's really her parents' place, so she gets … all … *(Gestures.)* You know. "Bitchy."

DOUG. That sucks. *(Beat.)* Jeez.

BETH. Yep. *(Beat.)* I wanna get outta here soon, actually, but … this city, right?

DOUG. I know.

BETH. *So* expensive.

DOUG. True.

BETH. Anyway … *(She trails off. Not finishing her thought. Shrugs her shoulders. Doug thinks for a moment, trying to fill in the gap.)*

DOUG. Yeah, "anyway." *(Beat.)* It was really nice before. Being with you.

BETH. Thanks.

DOUG. Honestly.

BETH. I believe you.

DOUG. Good! *Finally* ...

BETH. I never said I didn't believe you!

DOUG. I *know*, but ... you kinda got all ...

BETH. I just wondered why you stopped me at *that* moment. / When I was ...

DOUG. Okay. / I *know.*

BETH. That's all.

DOUG. But ... you understand why now? Right?

BETH. I guess.

DOUG. *Beth* ...

BETH. No, I guess I do, I get it ... I mean, I don't totally get it ...

DOUG. Because of our situation. That's why.

BETH. Same *situation* before we jumped into bed earlier tonight ...

DOUG. I know that!

BETH. Alright, well ... I'm just saying. The same dynamic was working then, too ... so ... we could've talked about it before now — or even back at the party ... on the train ... / at the front door ... on the stairs ...

DOUG. I *know*! / But ... it'd been so long since I'd seen you ... and ... you were ...

BETH. What?

DOUG. I don't know!! You looked beautiful and I was all ... I had the champagne toast at the gathering ... so ...

BETH. ... uh-huh ...

DOUG. ... and I looked across the room ... and I saw you there ... that was a great dress, by the way. / I'm no "fashion guy," but ... *damn* ...

BETH. Thanks. / No kidding! I don't think they could hardly believe it when you walked in with that t-shirt on *and* jeans! Ha!

DOUG. I know! *(Laughs.)* The look on their faces was kinda classic! *(Beat.)* Who makes that?

BETH. What, my dress? / Umm ... Narciso Rodriguez, I think. / No, from here. *He's* American.

DOUG. Yeah. / Is she Mexican? / Oh, it's a dude. Cool. *(Beat.)* Well, he did a good job!

BETH. I do like that dress.

DOUG. *Orange?* I mean ... that was ... nobody looked like you did! And your hair ...
BETH. Thanks.
DOUG. I love your hair ... I mean, ever since we were kids I loved your hair ...
BETH. That's sweet.
DOUG. First time I saw you — I can even remember that, seventh grade — you were new and we were all sitting there, in the lunchroom, and I saw you right off. The "new" kid.
BETH. Ha!
DOUG. What?! You were amazing-looking ... and ...
BETH. That's so lame ...
DOUG. I know it is! But ... you were ... and I saw you immediately and was just like ... *who is that girl?* She's cute and nice and ...
BETH. Huh. *(Beat.)* You never told me that.
DOUG. No, I know ... but still ... that's how it was. For me.
BETH. Oh.
DOUG. Anyway, your hair looked great. Not back in school — I mean yes, it looked great then, too, but — at the little ceremony thingie there at the church today ... I mean yesterday ... you looked incredible.
BETH. Thank you, Doug.
DOUG. No problem. It's the truth.
BETH. And you know I like that ...
DOUG. Yep!
BETH. So ...
DOUG. Yeah. So, so, so.
BETH. Now what?
DOUG. That's ... you tell me.
BETH. Ummmm ... *(Yawns.)* I really should get a bit more sleep.
DOUG. Right, no, you should! *(Beat.)* Damm, I'm really sorry ... see, I told you! I don't shut up sometimes — or just go in circles.
BETH. Totally okay.
DOUG. No, honestly ... that was stupid and, like, so self-centered on a work night! Sorry!
BETH. Not at all. *(Smiles.)* It was nice.
DOUG. Yeah?
BETH. Of course. Hearing lovely stuff about my hair and all that ... my *dress* ... it's very sweet. Thanks again.
DOUG. Absolutely. *(Beat.)* So ... yeah ... maybe it is worth jumping

back into bed for a little bit.

BETH. 'Kay. *(Beat.)* You coming?

DOUG. Ummmmm ... yeah, I could ... I guess ...

BETH. You make it sound *so* awful! / God!!

DOUG. No! / Come on!!

BETH. You do!!

DOUG. I'm just ...

BETH. What?! / It's not some prison sentence here...!

DOUG. I DON'T KNOW! / I KNOW THAT!

BETH. ... Guys have enjoyed the chance before ...

DOUG. I'm sure they have.

BETH. ... I'm not bragging, but ...

DOUG. "Guys"? Like, *hundreds* ... or...? / Was this an *army base* or something? The *Yankees*?

BETH. Ha! / SHUT UP!

DOUG. Just round it off if you wanna ...

BETH. Look who's talking!!

DOUG. What?

BETH. *You!*

DOUG. I'm not ... what? I've only ever fucked two Yankees in my life, so you're obviously not talking about me. *(Beat.) Kidding! (Beth is smiling but she's also being serious. She would be willing to pursue this but finally just shrugs. Doug looks at her, trying to read her. Finally he says:)* Look, I'm seriously lost now ... so ...

BETH. When you were a senior — *junior,* even! You were the one always jumping from person to person ...

DOUG. Yeah, but ... I'm ...

BETH. Is that not true?

DOUG. Just ... like ... that was just *dating* ...

BETH. So?

DOUG. I wasn't sleeping with 'em!

BETH. No?

DOUG. I mean ... not *all* of 'em! *(Beat.)* Not all at one time, anyway ...

BETH. Ha! *(Beat.)* And even now! You were all "Pam" and "Whitney" and like that ... and those're the recent ones!

DOUG. I'm not saying anything else. This is, like, totally *incriminating* here ...

BETH. You're the one saying it, not me!

DOUG. I know, but ...

BETH. Nobody forced you.

DOUG. Uh-uh, that's not true …

BETH. *Who?* Who forced you to date around all the time…?

DOUG. You did.

BETH. What?

DOUG. You made me do that.

BETH. What're you talking about…?

DOUG. Me. Not being able to date you.

BETH. No. *(Beat.)* That's not true …

DOUG. Of course … *(Beat.)* No one else has ever mattered … Right up until this very day. Because of *you*.

BETH. I didn't … know that.

DOUG. Well, now you do.

BETH. Huh.

DOUG. Yep. Learn a little something new every day.

BETH. I guess so.

DOUG. Not everybody. I mean, some people are just stupid and that's too bad — unable to learn, that's their lot in life — but most folks, yeah … we at least have the *capacity* for it. To learn something new. *(Beat.)* The possibility exists. Knowledge is our friend if we'll just give it a chance … *(Beat.)* I'll shut up now.

BETH. Yeah, that's probably true. *(Doug stands up, pointing toward the bedroom door. Beth looks at him and nods, getting to her feet, but kind of waiting, too. They let the moment linger. Getting closer to each other.)*

DOUG. … We probably shouldn't do this again …

BETH. No?

DOUG. I'm … I don't *think* so …

BETH. I'm trying not to think here. Right at this very moment …

DOUG. … but …

BETH. Shhhhhh. *(She leans in and kisses him again. Deeply. After a long moment, he responds. They continue for a few minutes, up against one wall of the apartment. Finally, Doug pulls away. Looks at Beth.)*

DOUG. *(Whispering.)* Oh boy …

BETH. I know.

DOUG. This is trouble. Seriously.

BETH. I realize that.

DOUG. Okay. So long as you do … *(They are only inches apart now. Touching. Teasing. Trying to stop but bodies remaining in contact.)*

BETH. Oh no, I totally get that part of it. I'm fully aware of the "trouble" aspect we've created here …

DOUG. Good.

BETH. And yet …

DOUG. I know. *(Smiling.)* I *know. (They kiss again. She starts to pull his shirt up and over his head.)* Hey … careful with the shirt … *(Beth smacks him in the stomach. Hard. He doubles over and laughs at the same time. Pulling his shirt down.)* Owww! I told you! / It's vintage!

BETH. What? / Such an ass…!

DOUG. All I asked for was that one thing — just be careful with the t-shirt!

BETH. *STAR WARS*! / God…!

DOUG. Come on! / It's *such* a good series! Can't believe you don't at least like Princess Leia … with the cute hair *thingies*! / She is *so* hot …

BETH. Stop … / I'm not even gonna get into this with you …

DOUG. Yeah, because it's impossible to defend the other side …

BETH. Shut up!

DOUG. *You* shut up!

BETH. No, you!

DOUG. You! / SHUT UP!!

BETH. YOU!! / *You* shut up or I'm telling Mom! *(Doug doesn't say anything in return — he simply looks at Beth with a strange expression on his face. She smiles and kisses him lightly. And again. And again. Doug kisses her back but he's also pulling back from her a bit. One more kiss and then they stop. Stepping away from each other but still touching. They both just stand there, unsure what to do next. Beth speaks first:)*

DOUG. … So. Fuck. Yeah. Mom. / And "Dad."

BETH. Yep. / Uh-huh.

DOUG. We probably should've broached this topic a little bit earlier, I guess.

BETH. "Broached" what?

DOUG. Everything. *(Beat.)* You know. You … me. *(Beat.)* Them. *(Beat.)* Mom and Dad. *(Beth doesn't say anything and doesn't take her hands off of Doug. She just looks deeper into his eyes.)*

BETH. I mean … let's be clear … My mom. Your dad.

DOUG. True. *(Beth kisses him on the cheek and then moves away. Plops down onto the couch again. Doug remains where he is. Up against the wall.)*

BETH. They're the ones who got us into this mess, right? I mean … in the first place. / Completely!

DOUG. Yeah … / agreed.

BETH. Your dad, really. I mean Mom was — my mom, I mean — she was just doing her thing and we moved into the neighborhood and it was your dad who was still married. Who sorta made the whole thing happen — not pointing any fingers but that's how it happened.
DOUG. No, I know! *(Beat.)* I was thinking about you as, like, I dunno … I wanted to ask you to one of the dances at school, or something like that … like, out to a movie, or a … whatever! A "date!" And then suddenly BAM! Everybody's upset and I'm trying to figure out what's going on … and then we're moving in together, all of us, because my mom is so pissed off and she's … it was nuts! I mean, that whole thing was just literally … insane. It was. That *summer*? Fuck.
BETH. I remember.
DOUG. Yeah. No, that's true … but so, it's not like we have, you know … the same blood thing or that sorta stuff going on … or even half or whatever.
BETH. Exactly.
DOUG. So, it's not … this isn't … the same as that. *(Beat.)* That's important. Right? It's *better.* I mean … technically … it's a *lot* better.
BETH. Uh-huh.
DOUG. But … still … They wanted us to be that way. To always act like brother and sister.
BETH. I know.
DOUG. Made sure we always behaved like that … insisted on it.
BETH. *Forced* us to.
DOUG. I had to watch over you … keep guys away from you. All that crap. "Brother" "sister" crap.
BETH. I *know*! Yes, of course … Even in my drunken state last night … I considered all that.
DOUG. You did?
BETH. Didn't *you*?
DOUG. I mean … yeah … *but* …
BETH. Ha! Not really …
DOUG. Kinda. *(Beat.)* And I kinda just wanted to go to bed with you … see you naked … / What?! I'm being totally honest here … that's what was mostly going on in my head. That thought. You naked. *(Robot voice.)* Must-See-Beth-Nude. Must-See-Beth-Nude. That was sorta all I was thinking at that point … last night.
BETH. You dick! / Yeah. Me, too. I mean you. Me seeing you that way. And you know … *(Grins.)* Yeah. Maybe without the weird robot voice.
DOUG. Right? *(Laughs.)* After all this time …

BETH. I *know*! *(Laughs.)* We had, like, two or three million opportunities as kids … in high school or whatnot … being left alone in the same house and our parents working or, like, late night … plus us being in the same city — any day over the past however long I could've just called you up, any *single* day — and yet *this* is how it happens. / *Right?*

DOUG. Pretty funny. / Yep. I mean *funny* is kinda relative, but … yeah. Probably shouldn't use the word "relative" right now, but … *(They both consider the situation at hand. How they have ended up here tonight.)*

BETH. Yeah. … They decide to renew their vows and then we … wow. That's kind of crazy. *(Beat.)* Right?

DOUG. Mmmm-hmmm.

BETH. I mean, don't you think?

DOUG. Yeah … I dunno … seeing you again … after I'm not even sure how long …

BETH. Probably … God, like, two years?

DOUG. Something like that.

BETH. It's gotta be at least that much. Two. That was about the last time we all did a Christmas together or Thanksgiving or that type of deal … / A holiday.

DOUG. Around there, yeah. / True. Out at the … ummmmm … lake house. *(Gestures.)* Yep.

BETH. I mean … not to be all *dramatic* or anything, but … you probably have no idea how hard I've worked at all this … how many times I've missed things, holidays or, like, get-togethers — those idiotic barbecues that Dad likes to have — so much stuff that I've steered clear of because I knew you were gonna be there or I thought maybe you would, just the *chance* that you might show up and so I found a reason to be out of town or on a plane or somewhere else. *(Beat.)* All of that was because of you.

DOUG. Same.

BETH. *What?*

DOUG. Same for me. / Of course! I missed tons of holidays or trips to the beach with everybody because I couldn't stand to see you. *(Beat.)* Obviously I *wanted* to … was *dying* to … but I stayed away. Thinking that it was sick and wrong or something, how you made me feel inside. At least some part of me did. Felt that way … *(Beat.)* But I also liked it, too, that it was sick and wrong, which then seemed sick … and wrong … See? I've thought about this a lot. I mean, a *lot* a lot.

BETH. Really? / Yeah. And then this stupid email comes — that they wanna "renew" their vows — I almost said "no" again.

DOUG. Me too!

BETH. Yeah, I was supposed to go to London for this conference thing … which I love … It's so nice over there … they always put us up in a really cute hotel and sometimes we get tickets to a musical even. / It's fun.

DOUG. Huh. / Never been.

BETH. No? *(Beat.)* We should go sometime …

DOUG. Yeah … that'd be … *(They look at each other for a second, each wondering just how a thing like that would work in the future.)*

BETH. Or not.

DOUG. No, I'd *love* that … it's just …

BETH. What?

DOUG. I dunno. *(He shrugs and looks away. Thinking. Beth watches him.)*

BETH. Doug, come on … what?

DOUG. It's … I mean … as what?

BETH. What does that mean?

DOUG. It means, "What would we go as?" *(Beat.)* Me and you … what are we now? After this…? *(Beat.)* I'm just saying: as this … here … whatever this is … or as like "bro and sis" or, or, or … what? / I'm curious.

BETH. Ummmmmmm … / A little early to label it, I'm thinking …

DOUG. No, but you know what I mean! Seriously!

BETH. Yeah, I do, but I'm saying let's just … whatever! Let's let the sun come up first before we worry about what our *Facebook* statuses are gonna be! *(Beat.)* Right?

DOUG. I guess.

BETH. … *Doug* …

DOUG. Well … I'm confused is all. / I am.

BETH. I know. / Me, too.

DOUG. Not very.

BETH. I am, too! Please don't tell me what I am right now … okay? *(Beat.)* OKAY? My last boyfriend was like that — I've had a couple who were — and I'm not gonna go back there again. Alright? I'm not. I am through dealing with assholes who wanna use me or tell me what to do, or … just, enjoy … *controlling* my life! *(Beat.)* Sorry, but …

DOUG. Got it.

BETH. Don't mean to get all heavy right now … but it's just a fact. *(Beat.)* Boyfriends and, like … at work … or even *Kim*.

DOUG. That's cool. Sorry if it felt like I was doing that.

BETH. No, I just …

DOUG. I wasn't.

BETH. Alright.

DOUG. I'm only trying to, you know … get, like, a *handle* on this …

BETH. Fine.

DOUG. That's all. *(Miming.)* Just wanna …

BETH. Understood. *(Beat.)* I'm sorry, too. Didn't mean to *snap* at you.

DOUG. Sure. *(He finishes the bottle of water and crushes it. Gets up and heads into the kitchen. Looking around.)*

BETH. You need something?

DOUG. Recycle? *(Beat.)* I'm sure "Kim" must …

BETH. Umm-hmm … first bottom cabinet, on the left. *(Doug nods and opens the cabinet. There are at least four bins marked with different labels. Pretty elaborate set-up for litter.)*

DOUG. Wow. / Is this for the whole building?

BETH. Yeah, I know. / Intense, right?

DOUG. God, who is this chick?! *(Reads.)* Plastics I'm guessing?

BETH. Yep. *(Doug tosses it into the appropriate bin and then closes the cabinet shut. He wanders back over toward Beth.)*

DOUG. She runs a pretty tight little ship here, seems to me.

BETH. God! You have no idea … she doesn't give a *shit* about the environment, but she's very into order in her own little world.

DOUG. Ha! Certainly seems that way …

BETH. It's kind of a nightmare, actually.

DOUG. I bet. *(Beat.)* You ever say anything? To her, I mean …

BETH. Oh, you know … once or twice, but … I'm basically stuck with it if I wanna stay.

DOUG. Yeah, but, I mean … technically half of this place is yours … so …

BETH. Yeah. "Technically." But try telling Kim that.

DOUG. I get it. *(Beat.)* Bummer. *(Doug plops back down on the couch. Beth moves over a bit.)*

BETH. Wish I could just pack my stuff up and not even be here when she gets back — that's my secret little fantasy thing I've got going most days in my head — but you know what it's like here.

DOUG. 'Course. It's hard. So you make sure you recycle and re-fluff the couch cushions when you stand up and never play your music too loud … and …

BETH. Ha! Have you *dated* Kim or something?!

DOUG. Nope! Not her, but let's just say I've seen the symptoms before … Kim is not entirely alone in her particular brand of … nearly … psychotic behavior.

BETH. Ha! Good to know!

DOUG. Yeah, I'm sure …

BETH. Which one?

DOUG. Excuse me?

BETH. Of your girlfriends … Pam or Whitney or which one … did that to you?

DOUG. Oh … you know … a couple, actually. I've had one or two close-calls with that type of girl …

BETH. Ha! Are you a slob? I don't remember you as a slob back home …

DOUG. No! *(Beat.)* I mean … *(He shrugs and says nothing — Beth waits. He continues.)* I'm just … whatever … normal … like a *normal* person who occasionally leaves a vintage t-shirt thrown over a chair and that sorta thing … / Good!

BETH. … completely acceptable in my book … / Even with an *Ewok* on it …

DOUG. Thank you! Yes! Bonus points for the Ewok reference. But seriously, it's what people do. When you're living your life and not sleeping in a museum or, or, or … some *palace* …

BETH. Exactly!

DOUG. I mean … seriously! That stuff can get a little bit ridiculous! *(Beat.)* Right?

BETH. I totally agree. *(Beat.)* Mom was the same way … remember?

DOUG. Oh course I do! *(Beat.)* But your mom, you mean, not mine … because mine was a fucking …

BETH. No, yeah. *My* mom. *(Beat.)* Of course.

DOUG. Yes. She was a little … intense … about it. About most things.

BETH. That's her!

DOUG. Yep. Like the hanging shoe racks, back of our closet doors … that was a little bit overpowering in ninth grade …

BETH. Ha! Yeah, those were … that was not your finest hour. Chore time.

DOUG. Oh God … I mean … who at that age cleans *baseboards* with any success? Seriously?!

BETH. Pine-Sol! Mom's drink of choice …

DOUG. No kidding! Lemon Pledge was her dirty little secret … *(They laugh together at this. Memories of their shared past. Doug touches Beth's face. Feels a piece of her hair. After a moment, Doug leans over and kisses Beth again. Softly. Tenderly.)* Listen … I don't wanna talk about them. / Not right now.

BETH. Okay. / That's …

DOUG. I mean, I don't *mind* … we *can*, but …

BETH. No, it's fine.

DOUG. … I'm … just …

BETH. What?

DOUG. I like you. *(Beat.)* There. Said it. *Again.*

BETH. Thanks. I like you, too …

DOUG. No, but I mean … seriously, though. I'm saying I *really* like you, Beth. / A lot.

BETH. I get it. / I *know.*

DOUG. You do?

BETH. Yeah. *(Beat.)* I mean, I can tell … *now.*

DOUG. Okay. Just wanted to make that clear. *(Doug waits and Beth looks over at him. She finally says:)*

BETH. And I said the same. In return.

DOUG. Yeah?

BETH. You heard me, right? So we'll just see, how it goes, I guess. Right?

DOUG. Oh. Okay.

BETH. I mean … *(Beth shrugs and doesn't know what else to say. Doug nods his head and touches her. Smiles weakly.)*

DOUG. No, that makes sense. It does.

BETH. You sure?

DOUG. Sure. Whatever.

BETH. No. Don't do that.

DOUG. I dunno what to say! I'm looking at you and … you know … I wanna dive back into bed with you, I do … that's what I *want.*

BETH. … okay …

DOUG. *But* I also … some part of me says that's an idiotic thing to be doing, even once more, unless we're, and then I start playing the whole "what if?" game in my head … and … and I can get pretty far, you know? I can take this pretty damn *far* if I let myself …

BETH. What's that … "what if?"

DOUG. Oh, come on! / Beth …

BETH. No, what? / *What?*

DOUG. "What if?" *(Beat.)* The hell do you think it sounds like…? *(Beat.)* WHAT-IF?

BETH. You mean … like…?

DOUG. Yes! *(Beat.)* "What if" we decided to give this a try? You and me?

BETH. As like…? / Oh. *(Beat.)* You mean like … shit. As a *couple*? That's what you're saying? "Us" as some permanent couple?

DOUG. Yes. / Yeah. *(Beat.)* As that. *(Beat.)* You've never thought that? / At *all*?

BETH. I mean, no, that's … / Fuck! That is a *much* bigger deal than … whatever we've done here. *(Beat.)* I mean … it is … *(Doug nods now, fully aware of what he's suggesting here.)*

DOUG. I know that.

BETH. … because … I'm …

DOUG. Beth, I *know*. Okay? I do. I get it. *(Beat.)* And yet you were all, like, "Hey, let's go to London … "

BETH. Yeah, but I wasn't saying as a "twosome" — and this isn't against you or an excuse or anything — but I don't know if I'm ready for that now. / Not right now. "Romance."

DOUG. Oh. / Okay. Alright. *(Beat.)* I see.

BETH. And I mean with *anybody*. *(Beat.)* I just … my last thing ended not so long ago, and it was bad — I mean, not "bad" bad but not great … not even close to being good — so I'm kinda … like … whatever … right now. *(Beat.)* Maybe not ready for too much.

DOUG. No, I get it …

BETH. And I thought you were still seeing somebody…?

DOUG. No … I mean … I am, but …

BETH. You are?

DOUG. Kind of.

BETH. But not seriously?

DOUG. No. *(Beat.)* Not *exclusively*.

BETH. I hate that, just so you know. Just so it's out there … "Not exclusively." That's a bullshit phrase.

DOUG. O-kay.

BETH. I mean it is, though, right? It is.

DOUG. I didn't say it because I thought that, but … you know …

BETH. No, I just mean … *really*? "Not exclusively"? That's like what a senator says to someone, or, like, how lawyers talk. / It doesn't mean anything. It's cowardly. / Please don't say that around me again … if you don't mind. "Not exclusively."

DOUG. Oh. / Wow. / Shit. *Alright…*

BETH. That's just how I feel about it.

DOUG. Yeah, well, luckily it doesn't seem to bother you too much …

BETH. *(Laughing.)* Ha! No … good thing I have *no* opinion on the subject!

DOUG. … somebody use that one on you recently?

BETH. Pretty much. *(Beat.)* Pretty much every man I've ever known … since birth.

DOUG. Got it. / Fair enough.

BETH. Alright? / Thanks.

DOUG. Anyway … I just meant that we're not like a steady thing anymore. *(Beat.)* Which *she* asked for … just to be clear. "Non-exclusive" was *her* idea. / *Hers.*

BETH. Okay. / Fine.

DOUG. So that's all. *(Beat.)* She *texted* it to me, actually, so …

BETH. Okay. I get it. / I understand it now.

DOUG. Good. / Alright.

BETH. I'm not seeing anybody … taking a break from all that. Like I said. For the *moment.* And that's why … I just can't really give you a response to what you said earlier.

DOUG. I understand.

BETH. Good. Thanks.

DOUG. Yep.

BETH. Thank you.

DOUG. … I didn't wanna see London *that* bad, anyway … if I want fish and chips I can always go over to Long John Silver's, I guess. *(Beat.) Fuck* England. *(He smiles at her and Beth smiles back at him. Slugs him a good one in the arm. He takes it and laughs.)*

BETH. You're *so* stupid …

DOUG. Yep.

BETH. Anyway … I just … *(Beat.)* Nothing. Don't worry about it.

DOUG. No, what?

BETH. It's no big deal.

DOUG. So tell me then.

BETH. Forget it.

DOUG. Come on. *(Waits.) Please.*

BETH. Look … I'm … what if I *did* want to? I mean, now that you've brought it up. What then? *(Beat.)* Hmmmm?

DOUG. "Want to" what?

BETH. You know.

DOUG. You mean…? *(Doug gestures, moving his hand from himself toward her. Beth nods and speaks again.)*
BETH. Yes. *(Beat.)* This. *(Beat.)* How would we even do that … I mean, tell people or deal with everything? 'Cause there'd be a *bunch* of everything … I mean, it would be a fucking shitshow, Doug.
DOUG. I dunno. We just would.
BETH. Yeah?
DOUG. Yes.
BETH. Okay, but *how*? Realistically?
DOUG. … you know … just by … I dunno.
BETH. Exactly. You-don't-know. You have no plan. *(Beat.)* If I did this I wouldn't be looking to do it for a "week," okay? Until *Christmas* … *(Beat.)* I want something real in my life for once. I want a partner and a home and love … like real, actual love. *(Beat.)* I deserve that. I *deserve* to be loved. / I do.
DOUG. I *know*! / Me too! Look, it'd take a while, I get that! Family and stuff … friends … everybody'd have something to say about it, I *know* that.
BETH. That's right. *Every*-body. Like, each and every person we know … / They would.
DOUG. … no, you're right … / I *know.*
BETH. *Everyone.*
DOUG. Okay, I get it! *(Beat.)* "All-people-everywhere." Even "Kim." *(They both smile at this and laugh out loud. Beth tries to imagine what Kim would think of their new arrangement.)*
BETH. Ha! *(Laughs.)* Kim *definitely* would … I don't even wanna think what Kim would have to say about it!
DOUG. Yeah, but, I mean … who cares?
BETH. Ummmmmmm …
DOUG. No, but literally … who?
BETH. *I* do! We both do … come on …
DOUG. I know, exactly — in the end — this is about *us*, not anybody else. Right? *(Beat.)* Isn't it?
BETH. Seriously, though … *Doug* … what would Dad say? *(Beat.)* You *know* what he'd say …
DOUG. He'd say a lot of stuff … a bunch of bullshit like always and *pontificate* about it and wave his hands … and, and …
BETH. … that's right …
DOUG. Because my dad is like that! A *talker*. A hypocrite and a talker. But let's be honest here. Is this worse that what he did? Did

42

several times, in fact? *(Beat.)* No … I'll answer that for you … no, it's not. *(Beat.)* Dad cheated on my mom, he did that — and not in some other city or, like, a different *country*, but right there. Where we lived. He did that and then, without blinking, he just slaps this new family together right in the same town and so we're all just supposed to deal with it … and okay, *fine*, but who says that *we* wouldn't've started dating if that hadn't happened … *(Seems like Beth is about to say something but she stops herself and Doug marches on.)* I told you I liked you! I told you that already … right as I first saw you — the *moment* I laid eyes on you. So who knows? Right? *(Beat.)* Who-knows. We only got together tonight because Dad cheated on Mom — *your* mom this time, not mine — / You knew that right? *(Beat.) Right?*

BETH. What? / I mean … I knew it was something … but …

DOUG. Well, that's *exactly* what it was! He is a cheater and so that's what he does. So he does that, they have a huge fight over it and, in the end, they decide to have this *thingie* last night — renew their vows rather than get a divorce … *That's* the kind of logic that desperate, middle-aged people have! *(Beat.)* That's a fact, Beth. *(Beat.)* And that little fact is why we are here, together, right now … it's because people do stupid shit like that, which makes no sense whatsoever. Zero. *None.*

BETH. … oh.

DOUG. So why is that *fine* — so normal and, I mean, natural in society today — that we all go eat cake and clap and raise some *bubbly* in their honor? Huh? *(Beat.)* Why can that happen but the fact that the two of us might get together — as adults and fully aware of the circumstances — who gets to say that what we're doing is so wrong or whatever? *(Beat.)* It just isn't … and that's all I mean by that. By saying "who cares what they think." *(Beat.)* Anyway, fine. I'm done. The-End.

BETH. Okay, but … *(Beat.)* Okay.

DOUG. … which means…?

BETH. Just "okay." You make a good point …

DOUG. *But?*

BETH. Nothing! *(Beat.)* I don't know what I'm thinking about all of it.

DOUG. *But* it's probably "no," right? / Right?

BETH. What is? / *What?*

DOUG. Us. *(Beat.)* What I'm hearing in your voice is "no" so just say it …

BETH. … Doug … come on …

DOUG. No, just so I'm prepared … *(Beat.)* Even with what happened tonight it's very likely to be a "no." Right? *(Beat.)* Just-say-it. You're gonna let me walk out of here and we're gonna *dream* about this, all the time, but in reality we'll stay away from each other, a few more years will pass until the next time that we allow ourselves to be around each other and then … whatever … it'll be too late. You'll be married, or I will … one of us will have a kid … and that'll be that … right? That's how people do it … that's the way we get by. *(Beat.)* Play it safe or wait a turn, or, or … whatever. Or *worse*. We run away. We give up. *(Beat.)* You know it's true. That's what we're about to do. We're gonna miss this chance and fuck it up … we are … I can see it happening.

BETH. … Maybe so. / For *right* now.

DOUG. No, we will. We *will*. / Shit. Be *honest*.

BETH. Okay, yeah! / *Yes!* / Maybe for always.

DOUG. Alright. / Okay. / Good. Get it? I got it.

BETH. But … that doesn't mean … you know …

DOUG. What?

BETH. That I don't care. About you.

DOUG. Sure.

BETH. Because I do …

DOUG. Great.

BETH. Okay. *(Beat.)* And we can even be … you know … "friends," maybe. Too.

DOUG. Okay. *(Beat.)* Fine. "Friends." *(Beat.) Cool.*

BETH. Don't do that. *(Beat.) Please.*

DOUG. No, I do, I get it. You care. Good. You don't have to say any more. Honestly. *(Beat.)* You're being so clear right now … loud and clear. Totally *loud* and *clear*. *(Beat.)* Just for the record, though … I didn't wanna just "get by." I wanted to change things. My life. Your life. *Us. (Doug stands and starts for the front door, but stops himself.)* … And I have no pants on.

BETH. Is that it?

DOUG. Hmmmm?

BETH. Are we done talking now? / Yeah?

DOUG. I guess … / Suppose so.

BETH. And you're what … are you going?

DOUG. I think I should.

BETH. Yeah?

DOUG. Probably.

BETH. Is that what you want?

DOUG. Ahhhhhh … under the circumstances … yeah. I guess.
BETH. Because why? Because I said we shouldn't get *engaged* right now? / Really?
DOUG. Something like that … / I just explained how I felt and I think it's best if I … whatever … get outta here now … is that okay?
BETH. …
DOUG. I should get back to my place. *(Beat.)* I mean, Since you aren't saying anything … *(Waits.)* Okay then. *(Beat.)* God, whatever. *(He starts off again toward the bedroom, but Beth stops him one more time.)*
BETH. You know … you don't *have* to take "no" for an answer …
DOUG. What's that mean?
BETH. It means you could fight for it. If you want me so badly … like you say …
DOUG. Beth … this isn't a *game* here … okay?
BETH. I know that.
DOUG. I'm not a game player … I'm not one of those guys … / Mr. "game" guy.
BETH. Nobody said that. / I'm not saying that to you. That it's a *game.*
DOUG. So then what?
BETH. So then I'm *scared,* alright?! I'm scared of what all this would mean — not just because of our friends or, or families even or any of that shit — I'm saying I am frightened of how I feel right now. About *this.*
DOUG. Oh. *(Beat.)* Okay.
BETH. I don't want you to go and I don't want you to stay and I don't think we can make it together, not in a relationship, and that's because of *me* probably more than it is you … but what I *really* want is for you to tell me that I'm wrong … *(Beat.)* Tell me that we *can* make a go of this … that we can do it if we try and that you're gonna spend the rest of your life making this all work out. Proving to me that we have a chance, because that's what I need … something stupid like that. I need *that,* if you really wanna know.
DOUG. That doesn't sound so stupid to me. I can do that …
BETH. But that's not what you did. I said "no" and you put your pants on to … go …
DOUG. … that's true … / But I was …
BETH. And that's what *every* guy I've ever been with has done! / The *same* fucking thing!
DOUG. But … That's not ME … I'm not those guys! I'd never walk out on you if we were together … You're so … from the first second

I saw you, I mean, *literally* … the very first, *years* ago … I'd never seen someone so … beautiful … so …

BETH. … So what.

DOUG. Really? "So what"?

BETH. Yeah … fuck yeah. So fucking what. My face. My body. So what? People walk out on pretty people all the time … *(Beat.)* You know how much shit I've taken in my life for this…? For something I had nothing to do with? Do you? People see this face and they think it's a *prize.* It's something to *win. To get.* I'm not a real person to them … I'm something to check off their fucking list … *(Beat.)* How's that sound for a way to spend your life? *(Beat.)* Hmmmm? *(Beat.) Doug? (Beat.)* Sound like fun?

DOUG. Geez … I mean no. *(Beat.)* … that sucks. *(Beat.)* Seriously.

BETH. Yeah. A little bit. Anyway, that's not what I need now. Somebody who thinks I'm "hot." Who wants to *see my tits.* I've done that … sorry. I can't do that again. I need someone who wants me. *ME. (Beat.)* I need somebody to put up a fuss. For me. I *need* that, Doug.

DOUG. Okay. You want a fuss, I'll make one … *(Does a little dance.)* See? I'm *fussing*! *(Does a little more.)* Look! This is *fuss*!

BETH. I'm *serious*!! What do I keep trying for? Putting myself out there for guy after guy after guy and for what … / for some … casual…?

DOUG. For nothing! / For no good reason.

BETH. It's just never been the right person, or at the right time or something. *(Beat.)* I'm not an unhappy person, but, you know, fuck … life can *really* … just … take it out of you …

DOUG. I agree. *(Beat.)* But just so you know: me either. *(Beat.)* I *mean* that. Honestly.

BETH. What?

DOUG. Never once. It's never been right. Or at least "right enough … " *(Beat.)* It doesn't mean it can't be, though.

BETH. I guess.

DOUG. I mean … I'm as cynical as the next guy or whatnot — that's maybe not true, maybe not like some of those morons out there on Twitter or whatever — but I still believe it can happen.

BETH. What can?

DOUG. You know. *(He shrugs his shoulders. Gestures. Beth takes this in.)*

BETH. Ahhhh. That.

DOUG. Yeah. That thing. The "L" word. / No!! Not *that* one. Come on. I mean "*love.*" / LOVE.

BETH. "Lesbian." / Oh. / *That* word.

46

DOUG. Yes. *(Beat.)* Just 'cause my dad turned it into a parlor game doesn't mean we have to believe that's how it works ...
BETH. I know, but it's ... so ... *corny* ... right? To talk like that ... about love or "The One." I mean ... isn't it? It's ... so ... stupid ... *(Beat.)* It feels stupid every time I say it ...
DOUG. Maybe so ... maybe it is, but who cares?! I know it probably is but seriously ... who the hell cares if people would laugh at us or think we're idiots for trying to make a go of this? I don't ... I'm not laughing one little bit ... *(Beat.)* Everyone's got to have an opinion about this stuff and I just feel like, I dunno, it drives me a little crazy, that's all. It does. *(Beat.)* So what? Who really gives a shit who you go out with — *(Beat.)* It sounds so obvious, I'm sure ... but look at us, worrying about this ... with *so* much else going on in the world! Like *actual* real problems! *(Beat.)* Listen, all I'm saying is this: Screw them, this is our thing, it's *our* business and it's all possible. It is. *(Beat.)* I could love you, Beth. / YES! *So* easily.
BETH. Yeah? / Huh.
DOUG. Like ... the *most* easy thing ever. Of all time.
BETH. Wow.
DOUG. Like "without training wheels" easy.
BETH. Ha!
DOUG. I mean this. *(Gets on one knee.)* See?
BETH. I can tell you do.
DOUG. So do it then! You asked me to fight for you and so I'm still here ... kneeling and begging you to go for it ... tonight. Do it.
BETH. Do what?
DOUG. Make a go of it with me! Don't mull this over or think about it or, or, like, make a list of pros and cons ... Let the good folks at Nike be your guide and just ... yeah. That's all I know to say ... If you're happy with all that other crap, trying again and again with people that you're "supposed" to be with, then keep on doing that ... but if you're ready for what's gonna be the best thing that you *ever* had in your life — that would be *me*, by the way, in case you had any trouble keeping up with my serpentine thoughts — which I warned you about — then you need to do this right now. Life is passing us by and I don't wanna lose another minute with you. Seriously. Not one more *second*. *(Beat.)* I promise to love you. For always. And not just your face or, like, your body ... I'll love *you*, Beth. I will.
BETH. ... and Mom and Dad...?
DOUG. They accept us or they don't.

BETH. Our friends?

DOUG. If they're *really* our friends then they jump on board … the rest we get rid of.

BETH. And…?

DOUG. What?

BETH. I dunno! *(Beat.) Kim?*

DOUG. You know what? *(Beat.) Fuck* Kim. *(Beth laughs out loud at this and grabs Doug with both of her hands. Kissing him on the mouth.)*

BETH. Honestly though …

DOUG. Just get some stuff together. I'll take care of Kim.

BETH. I mean … what? *(Beat.) Now?*

DOUG. *Right* now. This instant.

BETH. Doug …

DOUG. Beth.

BETH. I'm …

DOUG. Do this. Just *do* it. *(Beat.)* Go for broke. I'm begging you … *(Beth wavers for another moment. Unsure. Doug pulls her to him, kissing her again and again.)* This is me fighting for you, by the way. It doesn't get any better than this, just so you understand what's happening here. / Yep. Pretty much.

BETH. Ha! This is it, huh? / Good as it gets?

DOUG. Basically.

BETH. Okay then. *(Beat.)* I can live with that.

DOUG. Yeah … you'll find that most of my magic tapers off fairly quickly after this …

BETH. Good to know.

DOUG. Just wanted you to have all the facts up front …

BETH. Fair enough.

DOUG. Did I mention I'm crazy about you?

BETH. You didn't, actually … you said you *liked* me.

DOUG. Well, I did … just now. I said it, and I am. "Crazy-about-you." *(Beth laughs out loud, unable to contain herself. Doug smiles and laughs as well.)*

BETH. Oh shit … this is actually happening!

DOUG. If you'd get up off your ass, it is … *(Beat.)* Come on, let's go … before Kim gets back here and *shits* all over this!

BETH. … but, I mean …

DOUG. You might even get another hour or two of sleep if you hurry up. So, go grab some stuff! *(They look deeply into each other's eyes. A quiet moment.)*

BETH. *(Serious now.)* Doug … I'm really gonna go now … actually go into my room and pack my bags.

DOUG. Good. Go for it.

BETH. But, I mean, I *really* really am …

DOUG. I dare you to.

BETH. So … Doug, seriously … if you wanna stop me or anything … for any reason … do it right now. Immediately. *(Beat.)* Please do not break my heart here …

DOUG. GO.

BETH. *(Stepping away.)* I'm going … I'm *literally* walking away …

DOUG. So do it then.

BETH. But …

DOUG. Beth. *(Beat.) Now.*

BETH. Okay. Okay, I'm gonna do it. I am. I am going to pack my stuff.

DOUG. Not everything.

BETH. No?

DOUG. No! This is not "moving day."

BETH. Just enough for … what?

DOUG. Tonight. Tomorrow. This week. / It doesn't matter …

BETH. Alright. / Okay.

DOUG. Enough to run off with me and to make it real. That's all you need … nothing more.

BETH. Got it.

DOUG. So go already!

BETH. Going … *(Beth runs back and throws her arms around him one more time, then goes quickly to her room. Doug stands there for a beat, taking this all in. Smiles. He now moves into the kitchen. In an instant Beth is back outside her door, holding Doug's jeans and shoes in her hands.)* Are you totally sure? / No, but *totally* …

DOUG. BETH! / About what?

BETH. Us. The future. Everything.

DOUG. Yes.

BETH. You're "sure" sure?

DOUG. Yeah … for maybe the first time in my life … yes. I am.

BETH. Good. Me, too. *(Beat.)* "Ish." *(They smile at each other, then Beth moves over to a big stereo system on a shelf. Record player and speakers. She puts on some popular music — The Beatles or something good* — and then drops Doug's clothes on the couch. Heading off to*

---

* See Special Note on Songs and Recordings on copyright page.

her room. Doug appreciates the tunes for a moment. Listening. Doug turns back to the kitchen drawers. Starts rummaging around until he finds what he wants. He returns to the living area with something in one hand. He pulls out a piece and now it's clear what he has: one large roll of duct tape. Doug starts tearing off strips and putting them in place to spell out the word "Kim" on various objects. Her lamp and her coffee table and her couch, too. Beth enters the room — she stops dead, looking around at Doug's handiwork. She turns to him with a heart-breakingly beautiful smile. She goes to Doug. Throws her arms around him. They kiss.) That's the nicest present anybody ever gave me … "duct" tape, right?

DOUG. You remembered!

BETH. Yep!

DOUG. Yeah … *(Smiles.)* I think she'll get the point …

BETH. I bet she will … *(Doug goes to her and hands her the roll of tape. He nods toward the walls. Smiles.)*

DOUG. Wait. We're not done yet … *(Beth looks at him. Grinning. She suddenly runs and jumps on the couch and begins to plaster the wall with tape. It spells out the word "Kim." Doug works on some other area. After a bit they finish. Laughing. Exhausted. Kissing.)*

BETH. Fuck. You know what? You're *awesome* …

DOUG. Thanks. You too. *(Beat.)* Okay, let's get outta here …

BETH. Wait. *(Beat.)* I should turn on the stereo.

DOUG. Yeah, you should.

BETH. I really should …

DOUG. So do it then. Let it play.

BETH. Okay. I will. *(Beat.)* And thank you. *(During this exchange, Beth goes over to the stereo and puts on a different song. Something abrasive. She stands back and listens. Doug, too. This is beautiful noise.)*

DOUG. My pleasure. *(Beat.)* Don't get your hopes up for Christmases and birthdays, by the way … I'm not usually this clever …

BETH. You know what? I'll take what I can get.

DOUG. Fair enough. Me too.

BETH. Good. *(Beat.)* Just don't expect any … you know … naked handstands or anything …

DOUG. Ha! Never even entered my mind. *(Smiles.)* "Ish." *(Doug kisses Beth again. He stops and bends over, picking up her bags. He pretends to roll up the magazine with the American Apparel ad on it and tuck it into her things. Beth laughs and smacks him on the shoulder. He grins and holds out the paper for her. Beth rips the ad off of the magazine, crumples it up, tosses it into the living area. Together they take the rest of the paper and throw the pages into the air. They flutter slowly to the floor.)*

BETH. Here, Kim. Recycle *this*.

DOUG. You ready?

BETH. Yep.

DOUG. Yeah? / You sure?

BETH. Yes. / Uh-huh.

DOUG. Are you "sure" sure?

BETH. I am. *(Beat.)* I really really am.

DOUG. Then come on ... let's go *home* ... *(Doug grabs her bags while Beth leads the way toward the front door. She holds it open for him and he moves into the hallway. Exits. The music is still blaring. Beth looks around one last time. She takes a deep breath, smiles, and then steps out. Closing the door behind her. And the band plays on.)*

End of Play

PROPERTY LIST

Bottle of Smart Water
Books
Remote control
TV Guide magazine
Stereo and records
Pair of jeans and shoes
Large roll of tape
Bags

SOUND EFFECTS

Siren

NEW PLAYS

★ **A DELICATE SHIP by Anna Ziegler.** A haunting love triangle triggers an unexpected chain of events in this poetic play. In the early stages of a new relationship, Sarah and Sam are lovers happily discovering each other. Sarah and Nate know everything about each other, best of friends since childhood and maybe something more. But when Nate shows up unannounced on Sarah's doorstep, she's left questioning what and who she wants in this humorous and heartbreaking look at love, memory, and the decisions that alter the course of our lives. "Ziegler (who makes origami of time)… digs beneath the laughs, of which there are plenty, to plumb the pain that lurks below." –*Time Out (NY)*. [2M, 1W] ISBN: 978-0-8222-3453-1

★ **HAND TO GOD by Robert Askins.** After the death of his father, meek Jason finds an outlet for his anxiety at the Christian Puppet Ministry, in the devoutly religious, relatively quiet small town of Cypress, Texas. Jason's complicated relationships with the town pastor, the school bully, the girl next door, and—most especially—his mother are thrown into upheaval when Jason's puppet, Tyrone, takes on a shocking and dangerously irreverent personality all its own. HAND TO GOD explores the startlingly fragile nature of faith, morality, and the ties that bind us. "HAND TO GOD is so ridiculously raunchy, irreverent and funny it's bound to leave you sore from laughing. Ah, hurts so good." –*NY Daily News*. [3M, 2W] ISBN: 978-0-8222-3292-6

★ **PLATONOV by Anton Chekhov, translated by John Christopher Jones.** PLATONOV is Chekhov's first play, and it went unproduced during his lifetime. Finding himself on a downward spiral fueled by lust and alcohol, Platonov proudly adopts as his motto "speak ill of everything." A shining example of the chaos that reigned in his era, Platonov is a Hamlet whose father was never murdered, a Don Juan who cheats on his wife and his mistress, and the hero of the as-yet unwritten great Russian novel of his day. [9M, 4W] ISBN: 978-0-8222-3343-5

★ **JUDY by Max Posner.** It's the winter of 2040, and the world has changed—but maybe not by much. Timothy's wife has just left him, and he isn't taking it well. His sisters, Tara and Kris, are trying to help him cope while wrestling with their own lives and loves. The three of them seem to spend a lot of time in their basements, and the kids are starting to ask questions. This subterranean comedy explores how one family hangs on when technology fails and communication breaks down. "This smart, disturbing comedy is set…just far enough in the future to be intriguingly weird but close enough to the present to be distressingly familiar… Posner's revelations about this brave new world… waver between the explicit and the mysterious, and each scene… gives us something funny and scary to ponder." –*The New Yorker*. [3M, 3W] ISBN: 978-0-8222-3462-3

DRAMATISTS PLAY SERVICE, INC.
440 Park Avenue South, New York, NY 10016 212-683-8960
postmaster@dramatists.com www.dramatists.com

NEW PLAYS

★ **PLACEBO by Melissa James Gibson.** A minty green pill—medication or sugar? Louise is working on a placebo-controlled study of a new female arousal drug. As her work in the lab navigates the blurry lines between perception and deception, the same questions pertain more and more to her life at home. With uncanny insight and unparalleled wit, Melissa James Gibson's affectionate comedy examines slippery truths and the power of crossed fingers. "Smart, droll, beautifully observed…" –*New York Magazine.* "… subtle yet intellectually explosive…" –*TheaterMania.com.* [2M, 2W] ISBN: 978-0-8222-3369-5

★ **THE ROAD TO DAMASCUS by Tom Dulack.** As full-scale civil war rages in Syria, a bomb explodes in Manhattan and all roads lead to Damascus. A peace-seeking African Pope is elected to the Vatican and an Evangelical third-party president is in power in the U.S. With nuclear war looming, will the new Pope intervene directly in American foreign policy, or will he accede to the demands of Washington? Riddled with international intrigue, Tom Dulack's astonishingly prescient play imagines a world ripped from today's headlines. "Serious… satisfying… This near-future tale of an ill-conceived American plan feels authentic enough to have you believe that such events could take place any day. Or to remind you that similar ones have already occurred." –*NY Times.* [5M, 2W] ISBN: 978-0-8222-3407-4

★ **FOUR PLACES by Joel Drake Johnson.** When Peggy's two adult children take her out for lunch, they quietly begin to take apart her life. The drinks come fast, the tempers peak, the food flies. "… a meticulously structured work that captures a decades-long history of paralyzing family resentments, depleted affections, and sublimated cruelties in a single, uninterrupted 90-minute scene." –*Chicago Reader.* "FOUR PLACES is intense, remorseless drama at its finest." –*Backstage.* [1M, 3W] ISBN: 978-0-8222-3448-7

★ **THE BIRDS by Conor McPherson, from a story by Daphne du Maurier.** The short story that inspired Alfred Hitchcock's classic film is boldly adapted by Conor McPherson—a gripping, unsettling, and moving look at human relationships in the face of societal collapse. In an isolated house, strangers Nat and Diane take shelter from relentless masses of attacking birds. They find relative sanctuary but not comfort or peace; there's no electricity, little food, and a nearby neighbor may still be alive and watching them. Another refugee, the young and attractive Julia, arrives with some news of the outside world, but her presence also brings discord. Their survival becomes even more doubtful when paranoia takes hold of the makeshift fortress—an internal threat to match that of the birds outside. "Deliciously chilling… spring-loaded with tension…" –*Irish Independent.* "[McPherson] keeps us on the edge of our seat." –*Irish Times.* [2M, 2W] ISBN: 978-0-8222-3312-1

DRAMATISTS PLAY SERVICE, INC.
440 Park Avenue South, New York, NY 10016 212-683-8960
postmaster@dramatists.com www.dramatists.com

NEW PLAYS

★ **BUZZER by Tracey Scott Wilson.** Jackson, an upwardly-mobile black attorney, has just bought an apartment in a transitioning neighborhood in Brooklyn. He sees the potential of his old neighborhood, as does his white girlfriend Suzy… at first. When Jackson's childhood friend Don leaves rehab to crash with them, the trio quickly becomes trapped between the tensions inside their own home and the dangers that may lurk outside. "Skillful… [a] slow-burning, thought-provoking drama…" *–NY Times.* "[In BUZZER,] race is not a national conversation but an inner turmoil… the fact that the main gentrifier here is black turns the usual view of the subject inside out: Can one gentrify one's own home?" *–New York Magazine.* [3M, 1W] ISBN: 978-0-8222-3411-1

★ **THE NANCE by Douglas Carter Beane.** In the 1930s, burlesque impresarios welcomed the hilarious comics and musical parodies of vaudeville to their decidedly lowbrow niche. A headliner called "the nance"—usually played by a straight man—was a stereotypically camp homosexual and master of comic double entendre. THE NANCE recreates the naughty, raucous world of burlesque's heyday and tells the backstage story of Chauncey Miles and his fellow performers. At a time when it was easy to play gay and dangerous to be gay, Chauncey's uproarious antics on the stage stand out in marked contrast to his offstage life. "A nearly perfect work of dramatic art…" *–The New Yorker.* [4M, 4W] ISBN: 978-0-8222-3077-9

★ **EMPANADA LOCA by Aaron Mark.** Now living deep under Manhattan in an abandoned subway tunnel with the Mole People, a very hungry Dolores recounts her years selling weed with her boyfriend, her return to Washington Heights after thirteen years in prison, her fortuitous reunion with an old stoner friend who lets her give massages for cash in the basement under his empanada shop, and the bloodbath that sent her fleeing underground. Loosely inspired by the legend of Sweeney Todd, EMPANADA LOCA is contemporary Grand Guignol horror in the style of Spalding Gray. "Exuberantly macabre…" *–NY Times.* "Spine-tingling and stomach-churning…" *–Time Out (NY).* [1W] ISBN: 978-0-8222-3476-0

★ **SENSE OF AN ENDING by Ken Urban.** Charles, a discredited *New York Times* journalist, arrives in Rwanda for an exclusive interview with two Hutu nuns. Charged with alleged war crimes committed during the 1994 genocide, the nuns must convince the world of their innocence or face a lifetime in prison. When an unknown Tutsi survivor contradicts their story, Charles must choose which version of the truth to tell. Based on real events, SENSE OF AN ENDING shines a light on questions of guilt, complicity, and faith in the face of extreme violence. "A superb play… so intense that, in between each scene, you can hear the audience gulp for air." *–Time Out (London).* [3M, 2W] ISBN: 978-0-8222-3094-6

DRAMATISTS PLAY SERVICE, INC.
440 Park Avenue South, New York, NY 10016 212-683-8960
postmaster@dramatists.com www.dramatists.com

NEW PLAYS

★ **BETWEEN RIVERSIDE AND CRAZY by Stephen Adly Guirgis. Winner of the 2015 Pulitzer Prize.** Ex-cop and recent widower Walter "Pops" Washington and his newly paroled son Junior have spent a lifetime living between Riverside and crazy. But now, the NYPD is demanding his signature to close an outstanding lawsuit, the landlord wants him out, the liquor store is closed—and the church won't leave him alone. When the struggle to keep one of New York City's last great rent-stabilized apartments collides with old wounds, sketchy new houseguests, and a final ultimatum, it seems that the old days may be dead and gone. "Everyone's bound to be captivated by Guirgis's loudmouthed locals… [and] warm, rich dialect that comes right off the city streets." *–Variety.* [4M, 3W] ISBN: 978-0-8222-3340-4

★ **THE VEIL by Conor McPherson.** May 1822, rural Ireland. The defrocked Reverend Berkeley arrives at the crumbling former glory of Mount Prospect House to accompany a young woman to England. Seventeen-year-old Hannah is to be married off to a marquis in order to resolve the debts of her mother's estate. However, compelled by the strange voices that haunt his beautiful young charge and a fascination with the psychic current that pervades the house, Berkeley proposes a séance, the consequences of which are catastrophic. "… an effective mixture of dark comedy and suspense." *–Telegraph (London).* "A cracking fireside tale of haunting and decay." *–Times (London).* [3M, 5W] ISBN: 978-0-8222-3313-8

★ **ASHVILLE by Lucy Thurber.** Chronologically the second play in Lucy Thurber's The Hill Town Plays cycle, ASHVILLE is the story of Celia, sixteen years old and trapped in her poor white rural town, among people who can't hope for anything more than a good blue-collar job and a decent marriage. Celia wants something else in life, even if she can't articulate what that is. For a fleeting moment she thinks she finds the unnameable thing in her neighbor and tentative friend Amanda, but it may be that no one else can save Celia—only she herself can orchestrate her escape. "The best thing about these five plays is the detailed and quite devastating portrait they present of the depressed industrial region of western Massachusetts…" *–Variety.* [4M, 3W] ISBN: 978-0-8222-3355-8

★ **DOV AND ALI by Anna Ziegler.** Once upon a time, in the middle of a school, in the middle of Detroit, in the middle of the United States of America, there was a confused teacher and a precocious student. When Dov, an orthodox Jew, and Ali, a strict Muslim, get caught in a cultural crossfire, both are confronted with the same choice: Will they stand by their beliefs or face the devastating consequences? "… a flawless play… In a time of ceaseless snark and cynicism, its earnestness in asking bigger questions can be downright refreshing." *–NY Times.* "… an intense, intelligent and hugely promising play…" *–Guardian (UK).* [2M, 2W] ISBN: 978-0-8222-3455-5

DRAMATISTS PLAY SERVICE, INC.
440 Park Avenue South, New York, NY 10016 212-683-8960
postmaster@dramatists.com www.dramatists.com

NEW PLAYS

★ **EMERGING ARTIST GRANT by Angus MacLachlan.** Ethan, a successful independent filmmaker, is sweating over casting his newest project in his hometown of Winston-Salem when Spencer, a newly-minted adjunct theatre professor, auditions for the lead. Their mutual attraction is immediate, and they start a charming and amusing dance of personal and professional eroticism. Ethan's smart and witty older sister, Liz, is thrown into the mix. She supports herself as a hairdresser; her acting career, and her hopes, have derailed a bit with time. A subtly comedic story set in the creative world, EMERGING ARTIST GRANT explores how we struggle to make something of our lives, and it questions the moral crises we encounter when trying for our dreams. "… [A] witty play [and] something of a master class in artistic self-appraisal and survival… the questions of how many interpersonal boundaries are transgressed… remain up in the air until the end." –*IndyWeek.com.* [1M, 2W] ISBN: 978-0-8222-3365-7

★ **THE BELLE OF AMHERST by William Luce.** In her Amherst, Massachusetts, home, the reclusive nineteenth-century poet Emily Dickinson recollects her past through her work, her diaries and letters, and a few encounters with significant people in her life. "William Luce has chiseled a perfectly detailed cameo… He has made an Emily so warm, human, loving and lovable that her ultimate vulnerability will break your heart." –*Boston Globe.* [1W] ISBN: 978-0-8222-3373-2

★ **LET ME DOWN EASY by Anna Deavere Smith.** In this solo show constructed from verbatim interview transcripts, Anna Deavere Smith examines the miracle of human resilience through the lens of the national debate on health care. After collecting interviews with over 300 people on three continents, Smith creates an indelible gallery of 20 individuals, known and unknown—from a rodeo bull rider and a World Heavyweight boxing champion to a New Orleans doctor during Hurricane Katrina, as well as former Texas Governor Ann Richards, cyclist Lance Armstrong, film critic Joel Siegel, and supermodel Lauren Hutton. A work of emotional brilliance and political substance from one of the treasures of the American theater. Originally created as a one-person show, the author encourages multi-actor productions of the play. "It's stunning, beautiful, and transcendent." –*SF Weekly.* [1W] ISBN: 978-0-8222-2948-3

★ **PORT AUTHORITY by Conor McPherson.** PORT AUTHORITY follows three generations of Irishmen as they tell the stories of their lives. "Overwhelmingly poignant…McPherson rivetingly shows how the past is in all our presents." –Evening Standard (London). "McPherson occupies his familiar terrain with glittering wit and assurance… he writes like a recording Irish angel…[with] a poetic understanding of what might have been." –*Guardian (UK).* [3M] ISBN: 978-0-8222-3311-4

DRAMATISTS PLAY SERVICE, INC.
440 Park Avenue South, New York, NY 10016 212-683-8960
postmaster@dramatists.com www.dramatists.com

NEW PLAYS

★ **BRIGHT HALF LIFE by Tanya Barfield.** A moving love story that spans decades in an instant—from marriage, children, skydiving, and the infinite moments that make a life together. "BRIGHT HALF LIFE, a sixty-five minute chronicle of a deeply committed lesbian relationship, is contemporary as a play could be but the theme is classic and timeless… the presentation of the highs and lows of coupledom, as exampled in this piece, defy the ages." *–Huffington Post.* [2W] ISBN: 978-0-8222-3351-0

★ **WAIT UNTIL DARK by Frederick Knott, adapted by Jeffrey Hatcher.** Forty-seven years after *Wait Until Dark* premiered on Broadway, Jeffrey Hatcher has adapted Frederick Knott's 1966 original, giving it a new setting. In 1944 Greenwich Village, Susan Hendrix, a blind yet capable woman, is imperiled by a trio of men in her own apartment. As the climax builds, Susan discovers that her blindness just might be the key to her escape, but she and her tormentors must wait until dark to play out this classic thriller's chilling conclusion. "… reminds CGI-infected audiences that a few shadows, a shiny knife, and compelling characters can still go a long way to create suspense… WAIT UNTIL DARK earns its climax through enthralling, layered characters." *–Entertainment Weekly.* [4M, 2W] ISBN: 978-0-8222-3205-6

★ **BAKERSFIELD MIST by Stephen Sachs.** Maude, a fifty-something un-employed bartender living in a trailer park, has bought a painting for a few bucks from a thrift store. Despite almost trashing it, she's now convinced it's a lost masterpiece by Jackson Pollock worth millions. But when world-class art expert Lionel Percy flies over from New York and arrives at her trailer home in Bakersfield to authenticate the painting, he has no idea what he is about to discover. Inspired by true events, this hilarious and thought-provoking new comedy-drama asks vital questions about what makes art and people truly authentic. "A triumph! Hugely gratifying! An absorbing, hilarious two-hander about the nature of art and the vagaries of human perception." *–Backstage.* "Sachs' short, clever play is a battle of wits." *–NY Times.* [1M, 1W] ISBN: 978-0-8222-3280-3

★ **SWITZERLAND by Joanna Murray-Smith.** Somewhere in the Swiss Alps, grande dame of crime literature Patricia Highsmith lives with an impressive collection of books, and a somewhat sinister collection of guns and knives. She finds solace in her solitude, her cats, and cigarettes. But when a mysterious international visitor arrives at her perfectly secluded home, her love of fictional murders becomes a dangerous reality. "[SWITZERLAND] explores what it's like to be a woman writer in a man's literary kingdom… Murray-Smith's dialogue sparkles with witty one-liners and delicious snark…" *–Time Out (Sydney).* [1M, 1W] ISBN: 978-0-8222-3435-7

DRAMATISTS PLAY SERVICE, INC.
440 Park Avenue South, New York, NY 10016 212-683-8960
postmaster@dramatists.com www.dramatists.com